Sasha Fenton's
Rising Signs

To Steve
with love from
Sasha Fent

Sasha Fenton's
Rising Signs

Discover how you appear to others

ZAMBEZI PUBLISHING LTD

Published in 2009 by
Zambezi Publishing Ltd
P.O. Box 221 Plymouth, Devon PL2 2YJ (UK)
web: www.zampub.com email: info@zampub.com

Text: copyright © 2009 Sasha Fenton
Cover design: copyright © 2009 Jan Budkowski
Text sketches: copyright © 2009 Jonathan Dee
Astro charts created in Solar Fire™
Certain images/part-images, on cover and within:
with much appreciation, courtesy of NASA.

Sasha Fenton has asserted her moral right
to be identified as the author of this work in terms of
the Copyright, Designs and Patents Act 1988.
British Library Cataloguing-in-Publication Data:
A catalogue record for this book is available from
the British Library

Typeset by Zambezi Publishing Ltd, Plymouth UK
Printed and bound in the UK by Lightning Source (UK) Ltd
ISBN-13: 978-1-903065-75-4

About the Author

Sasha became a professional consultant astrologer in 1973, but had to tail off her consultancy business once her writing took off. She has written over 120 books, mainly on mind, body and spirit subjects, with sales of around 6.5 million copies to her credit, and translations of some titles into a dozen languages. Sasha wrote the stars columns for several British newspapers and magazines, and contributed a chapter to "Llewellyn's Sun Sign Book" every year for ten years.

Having broadcast regularly all over the UK and in several other countries at times, she has also lectured widely, including festivals in various parts of the UK and Sydney, Melbourne, Johannesburg and Cape Town.

Sasha has been President of the British Astrological and Psychic Society (BAPS), Chair and Treasurer for the British Advisory Panel on Astrological Education (APAE), and a member of the Executive Council of the Writers' Guild of Great Britain.

Sasha's first husband, Tony Fenton, died of cancer and diabetes related problems. She met her second husband, Jan Budkowski, in South Africa and their first home was a tent on the banks of the Zambezi River in Jan's country of birth, Zambia. They married and settled in the west of England, where they now run Zambezi Publishing Ltd. Sasha has two children and two granddaughters.

Other books by the author

Astrology
Sun Signs
Rising Signs
Moon Signs
Understanding Astrology
How to Read Your Star Signs
Astrology... on the Move!
Astrology for Wimps
Reading the Future
Astrology for Living
The Hidden Zodiac
Astrology: East and West
The Planets
What Time Were You Born?
Understanding the Astrological Vertex
Ten years' contribution to Llewellyn's Sun
Sign Book
Sasha Fenton's Moon SIgns

With Jonathan Dee
The Moon Sign Kit
Your Millennium Forecasts
Forecasts 2001
Forecasts 2002
Sun Signs Made Simple
Six sets of twelve Astro-guides – from
1995 to 2000

Palmistry
With illustrator, Malcolm Wright
The Living Hand
Hand Reading
Simply Palmistry
Modern Palmistry
Living Palmistry
Learning Palmistry
The Book of Palmistry

Tarot
Fortune-Telling by Tarot Cards
Tarot in Action!
Super Tarot
Elementary Tarot
The Tarot

Chinese
Elementary I Ching

Chinese Divinations
Feng Shui for the Home

Psychic and Fortune Telling
The Fortune-Teller's Workbook
The Aquarian Book of Fortune Telling
The Book of Spells
Star*Date*Oracle
(with Jonathan Dee)
Body Reading
The Fortune Teller's Handbook
Tea Cup Reading
Dreams
(with Jan Budkowski)
How to Be Psychic
Dream Meanings
Fortune-Telling by Tea Leaves
Simply Chakras

Money and Business
Prophecy for Profit
(with Jan Budkowski)
The Money Book
(with Jan Budkowski)

Health
Diabetes: An Everyday Guide

Upcoming New Titles
The Love Tarot
The Flying Stars

Upcoming Revised Titles
Sasha Fenton's Planets
Body Reading
Understanding Astrology

Contents

This Book's Natal Chart

(i.e. its publication date):

Plymouth,

14th June, 2009

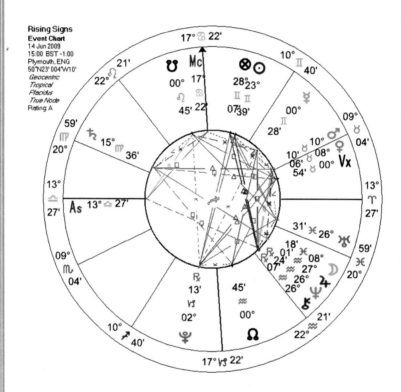

Rising Signs
Event Chart
14 Jun 2009
15:00 BST -1:00
Plymouth, ENG
50°N23' 004°W10'
Geocentric
Tropical
Placidus
True Node
Rating: A

1

The Rising Sign and the Ascendant

The Outer Manner

The rising sign frequently rules a person's outer manner, mindset and career choices, but this isn't an absolute rule. One can argue that the rising sign represents the kind of person our parents, teachers and childhood friends wanted us to be, while the Sun, Moon and other planets show our true selves.

Many of us project the ascendant when we are in new situations. We often choose to use it as a shield that hides and protects the real personality, thereby allowing us to assess a new situation before revealing our true feelings. It would be terrific if astrologers could categorically say that the rising sign invariably rules the outer manner and appearance, but, as in other areas of life, few things are cast in stone. Nevertheless, the rising sign is fascinating.

The ascendant is so important, that without knowing exactly what is rising, the astrologer is partially working in the dark. If nothing else, an exact ascendant marks the starting point of the astrological houses and it sets the position of such astrological features as the descendant, midheaven, Immum Coeli, part of fortune, east point, vertex and much else.

Are the Ascendant and Rising Sign the Same Thing?
The terms are often used interchangeably, but the ascendant refers to the *exact position* within the rising sign. For instance, you might have had Taurus rising when you were born, but your ascendant may be 18 degrees of Taurus.

Definitions
The rising sign is the sign of the zodiac appearing on the eastern horizon at the time of birth. The ascendant is the exact degree of the rising sign at birth.

Appearance

Many people look far more like their rising sign than their Sun sign, while others are a combination of both. However, there are people whose appearance is strongly influenced by other factors on their birthchart, along with inherited factors, such as race, colour and family likeness.

Several years ago, I read of a survey that had been carried out with 100 subjects. About 45 per cent looked like their Sun sign and about another 40 per cent resembled their rising sign, while the remainder looked like either their Moon sign or the sign in which their chart ruler was placed. The chart ruler is the planet associated with the rising sign. For example, in the case of Libra rising, the ruling planet is Venus. I'm not sure that one survey of 100 people proves much, but it's interesting. It's possible that the outward projection of the rising sign is more apparent in our mannerisms and behaviour than our looks. I've noticed that, whenever I or any other astrologer has been daft enough to try and guess a person's Sun sign, more often we come up with their rising sign.

It's always interesting to take a look at a family group to see how the signs are distributed within it. Frequently, one person's Sun is the rising sign of another and the Moon sign or the MC of yet a third. It's also interesting to note the factors on the birthcharts of close associates to see whether they connect with our Sun, Moon, Asc, Dsc, MC or IC.

Do We Outgrow Our Rising Sign?

There is a theory that many people are far more like their Moon sign or their rising sign during the first thirty years, becoming more like their Sun sign later on. Another theory is that the progression of the ascendant from one sign to the next weakens the rising sign's influence and allows the subject to grow and change. These are both worthwhile theories, as long as you are flexible about them and don't consider them to be written in tablets of stone.

Signs of Long and Short Ascension

During the course of a 24-hour day in the tropics, the signs rise at more or less two hourly intervals, but the further away one moves from the equator the more distorted this movement becomes. This means that at certain times of the year in Britain, we can see the sign of Cancer taking as much as two-and-three-quarter hours to rise over the horizon, while at certain times of the year, Pisces will take little more than twenty minutes to do so.

Therefore, in our part of the world, it's far easier to find people who have the longer ascension signs of Cancer and Leo rising than the shorter ascension signs of Pisces or Aries. In the southern hemisphere, the signs of longest ascension are Capricorn and Aquarius, while the shorter signs are Virgo and Libra.

Abbreviations

Some of the astrological abbreviations in this book are:

Ascendant:	Asc
Descendant:	Dsc
Medium Coeli/midheaven:	MC
Immum Coeli/nadir:	IC

2

Finding Your Rising Sign

The rising sign finder table that you will see in a moment is suitable for births in any part of the world. This will give you a fairly accurate rising sign, unless you are on the cusp of two signs, in which case, read both of them in this book and you will soon see which one applies to you. You can learn more about times of birth from my book, 'What Time Were You Born'.

N.B: If you were born in the UK during British Summer Time (BST), or elsewhere during Daylight Saving Time, please deduct one hour from your time of birth.

Sooner or later, you will want to know the exact location of your ascendant (the exact degree of the sign that was rising). You can find this initially by finding and using one of the free astro services on the Internet, such as the one currently available on the Astro.com website.

Things change, however, but a Google search for terms such as "free astro chart" will find what's on tap. You could visit an astrologer, send off to Equinox for computerised chart and report, or you could buy your own astrology software. Amazon.co.uk sometimes carries amazingly inexpensive, effective and easy-to-use software packages, but again, things change, so you need to look for yourself. I try to keep some suggestions up to date on my website (sashafenton.com), but an up-to-date web search is always the best idea.

The Quick and Easy Rising Sign Finder

Birthdate	Aries	Taurus	Gemini
ARI 21 to 31 Mar	5.30am to 6.29am	6.30am to 7.44am	7.45am to 9.29am
01 to 10 Apr	5.00am to 5.59am	6.00am to 7.14am	7.15am to 8.59am
11 to 20 Apr	4.15am to 5.14am	5.15am to 6.29am	6.30am to 8.14am
TAU 21 to 30 Apr	3.30am to 4.29am	4.30am to 5.44am	5.45am to 7.29am
01 to 10 May	3.00am to 3.59am	4.00am to 5.14am	5.15am to 6.59am
11 to 21 May	2.30am to 3.29am	3.30am to 4.44am	4.45am to 6.29am
GEM 22 to 31 May	2.00am to 2.59am	3.00am to 4.14am	4.15am to 5.59am
01 to 10 Jun	1.30am to 2.29am	2.30am to 3.44am	3.45am to 5.29am
11 to 21 Jun	12.45am to 1.44am	1.45am to 2.59am	3.00am to 4.44am
CAN 22 to 30 Jun	12.00am to 12.59am	1.00am to 2.14am	2.15am to 3.59am
01 to 11 Jul	11.30pm to 12.29am	12.30am to 1.44am	1.45am to 3.29am
12 to 22 Jul	11.00pm to 11.59pm	12.00am to 1.14am	1.15am to 2.59am
LEO 23 to 31 Jul	9.45pm to 10.44pm	10.45pm to 1.59pm	12.00am to 1.44am
01 to 11 Aug	9.15pm to 10.14pm	10.15pm to 11.29pm	1.30pm to 1.14am
12 to 23 Aug	8.30pm to 9.29pm	9.30pm to 10.44pm	10.45pm to 12.29am
VIR 24 to 31 Aug	7.30pm to 8.29pm	8.30pm to 9.44pm	9.45pm to 11.29pm
01 to 11 Sep	7.00pm to 7.59pm	8.00pm to 9.14pm	9.15pm to 10.59pm
12 to 22 Sep	6.15pm to 7.14pm	7.15pm to 8.29pm	8.30pm to 10.14pm
LIB 23 to 30 Sep	5.30pm to 6.29pm	6.30pm to 9.44pm	9.45pm to 11.29pm
01 to 11 Oct	5.00pm to 5.59pm	6.00pm to 7.14pm	7.15pm to 8.59pm
12 to 23 Oct	4.15pm to 5.14pm	5.15pm to 6.29pm	6.30pm to 8.14pm
SCO 24 to 31 Oct	3.30pm to 4.29pm	4.30pm to 5.44pm	5.45pm to 7.29pm
01 to 11 Nov	2.45pm to 3.44pm	3.45pm to 4.59pm	5.00pm to 6.44pm
12 to 22 Nov	2.15pm to 3.14pm	3.15pm to 4.29pm	4.30pm to 6.14pm
SAG 23 to 30 Nov	1.30pm to 2.29pm	2.30pm to 3.44pm	3.45pm to 5.29pm
01 to 11 Dec	12.45pm to 1.44pm	1.45pm to 2.59pm	3.00pm to 4.44pm
12 to 21 Dec	12.15pm to 1.14pm	1.15pm to 2.29pm	2.30pm to 4.14pm
CAP 22 to 31 Dec	11.15am to 12.14pm	12.15pm to 1.29pm	1.30pm to 3.14pm
01 to 11 Jan	10.45am to 11.44am	11.45am to 12.59pm	1.00pm to 2.44pm
12 to 20 Jan	10.15am to 11.14am	11.15am to 12.29pm	12.30pm to 2.14pm
AQU 21 to 31 Jan	9.30am to 10.29am	10.30am to 11.44am	11.45am to 1.29pm
01 to 10 Feb	9.00am to 9.59am	10.00am to 11.14am	11.15am to 12.59pm
11 to 18 Feb	8.15am to 9.14am	9.15am to 10.29am	10.30am to 12.14pm
PIS 19 to end Feb	7.30am to 8.29am	8.30am to 9.44am	9.45am to 11.29am
01 to 10 Mar	7.15am to 8.14am	8.15am to 9.29am	9.30am to 11.14am
11 to 20 Mar	6.30am to 7.29am	7.30am to 8.44am	8.45am to 10.29am

Birthdate	Cancer	Leo	Virgo
ARI 21 to 31 Mar	9.30am to 11.59am	12.00pm to 2.44pm	2.45pm to 5.29pm
01 to 10 Apr	9.00am to 11.29am	11.30am to 2.14pm	2.15pm to 4.59pm
11 to 20 Apr	8.15am to 10.44am	10.45am to 1.29pm	1.30pm to 4.14pm
TAU 21 to 30 Apr	7.30am to 9.59am	10.00am to 12.44pm	12.45pm to 3.29pm
01 to 10 May	7.00am to 9.29am	9.30am to 12.14pm	12.15pm to 2.59pm
11 to 21 May	6.30am to 8.59am	9.00am to 11.44am	11.45am to 2.29pm
GEM 22 to 31 May	6.00am to 8.29am	8.30am to 11.14am	11.15am to 1.59pm
01 to 10 Jun	5.30am to 7.59am	8.00am to 10.44am	10.45am to 1.29pm
11 to 21 Jun	4.45am to 7.14am	7.15am to 9.59am	10.00am to 12.44pm
CAN 22 to 30 Jun	4.00am to 6.29am	6.30am to 9.14am	9.15am to 11.59am
01 to 11 Jul	3.30am to 5.59am	6.00am to 8.44am	8.45am to 11.59am
12 to 22 Jul	3.00am to 5.29am	5.30am to 8.14am	8.15am to 10.59am
LEO 23 to 31 Jul	1.45am to 4.00am	4.15am to 6.59am	7.00am to 9.44am
01 to 11 Aug	1.15am to 3.44am	3.45am to 6.29am	6.30am to 9.14am
12 to 23 Aug	12.30am to 2.59am	3.00am to 5.44am	5.45am to 8.29am
VIR 24 to 31 Aug	11.30pm to 1.59am	2.00am to 4.44am	4.45am to 7.29am
01 to 11 Sep	11.00pm to 1.29am	1.30am to 4.14am	4.15am to 6.59am
12 to 22 Sep	10.15pm to 12.44am	12.45am to 3.29am	3.30am to 6.14am
LIB 23 to 30 Sep	9.30pm to 11.59pm	12.00am to 2.44am	2.45am to 5.29am
01 to 11 Oct	9.00pm to 11.29pm	11.30pm to 2.14am	2.15am to 4.59am
12 to 23 Oct	8.15pm to 10.44pm	10.45pm to 1.29am	1.30am to 4.14am
SCO 24 to 31 Oct	7.30pm to 9.59pm	10.00pm to 12.44am	12.45am to 3.29am
01 to 11 Nov	6.45pm to 9.14pm	9.15pm to 11.59pm	12.00am to 2.44am
12 to 22 Nov	6.15pm to 8.44pm	8.45pm to 11.29pm	11.30pm to 2.14am
SAG 23 to 30 Nov	5.30pm to 7.59pm	8.00pm to 10.44pm	10.45pm to 1.29am
01 to 11 Dec	4.45pm to 7.14pm	7.15pm to 9.59pm	10.00pm to 12.44am
12 to 21 Dec	4.15pm to 6.44pm	6.45pm to 9.29pm	9.30pm to 12.14am
CAP 22 to 31 Dec	3.15pm to 5.44pm	5.45pm to 8.29pm	8.30pm to 11.14pm
01 to 11 Jan	2.45pm to 5.14pm	5.15pm to 7.59pm	8.00pm to 10.44pm
12 to 20 Jan	2.15pm to 4.44pm	4.45pm to 7.29pm	7.30pm to 10.14pm
AQU 21 to 31 Jan	1.30pm to 3.59pm	4.00pm to 6.44pm	6.45pm to 9.29pm
01 to 10 Feb	1.00pm to 3.29pm	3.30pm to 6.14pm	6.15pm to 8.59pm
11 to 18 Feb	12.15pm to 2.44pm	2.45pm to 5.29pm	5.30pm to 8.14pm
PIS 19 to end Feb	11.30am to 1.59pm	2.00pm to 4.44pm	4.45pm to 7.29pm
01 to 10 Mar	11.15am to 1.44pm	1.45pm to 4.29pm	4.30pm to 7.14pm
11 to 20 Mar	10.30am to 12.59pm	1.00pm to 3.44pm	3.45pm to 6.29pm

Birthdate	Libra	Scorpio	Sagittarius
ARI 21 to 31 Mar	5.30pm to 8.14pm	8.15pm to 10.59pm	11.00pm to 1.29am
01 to 10 Apr	5.00pm to 7.44pm	7.45pm to 10.29pm	10.30pm to 12.59am
11 to 20 Apr	4.15pm to 6.59pm	7.00pm to 9.44pm	9.45pm to 12.14am
TAU 21 to 30 Apr	3.30pm to 6.14pm	6.15pm to 8.59pm	9.00pm to 11.29pm
01 to 10 May	3.00pm to 5.44pm	5.45pm to 8.290pm	8.30pm to 10.59pm
11 to 21 May	2.30pm to 5.14pm	5.15pm to 7.59pm	8.00pm to 10.29pm
GEM 22 to 31 May	2.00pm to 4.44pm	4.45pm to 7.29pm	7.30pm to 9.59pm
01 to 10 Jun	1.30pm to 4.14pm	4.15pm to 6.59pm	7.00pm to 9.29pm
11 to 21 Jun	12.45pm to 3.29pm	3.30pm to 6.14pm	6.15pm to 8.44pm
CAN 22 to 30 Jun	12.00pm to 2.44pm	2.45pm to 5.29pm	5.30pm to 7.59pm
01 to 11 Jul	11.30am to 2.14pm	2.15pm to 4.59pm	5.00pm to 7.29pm
12 to 22 Jul	11.00am to 1.44pm	1.45pm to 4.29pm	4.30pm to 6.59pm
LEO 23 to 31 Jul	9.45am to 12.29pm	12.30pm to 3.14pm	3.15pm to 5.44pm
01 to 11 Aug	9.15am to 11.59am	12.00pm to 2.44pm	2.45pm to 5.14pm
12 to 23 Aug	8.30am to 11.14am	11.15am to 1.59pm	2.00pm to 4.29pm
VIR 24 to 31 Aug	7.30am to 10.14am	10.15am to 12.59pm	1.00pm to 3.29pm
01 to 11 Sep	7.00am to 9.44am	9.45am to 12.29pm	12.30pm to 2.59pm
12 to 22 Sep	6.15am to 8.59am	9.00am to 11.14am	11.45am to 2.14pm
LIB 23 to 30 Sep	5.10am to 8.14am	8.15am to 10.59am	11.00am to 1.29pm
01 to 11 Oct	5.00am to 7.44am	7.45am to 10.29am	10.30am to 12.59pm
12 to 23 Oct	4.15am to 6.59am	7.00am to 9.44am	9.45am to 12.14pm
SCO 24 to 31 Oct	3.30am to 6.14am	6.15am to 8.59am	9.00am to 11.29am
01 to 11 Nov	2.45am to 5.29am	5.30am to 8.14am	8.15am to 10.44am
12 to 22 Nov	2.15am to 4.59am	5.00am to 7.44am	7.45am to 10.14am
SAG 23 to 30 Nov	1.30am to 4.14am	4.15am to 6.59am	7.00am to 9.29am
01 to 11 Dec	12.45am to 3.29am	3.30am to 6.14am	6.15am to 8.44am
12 to 21 Dec	12.15am to 2.59am	3.00am to 5.44am	5.45am to 8.14am
CAP 22 to 31 Dec	11.15pm to 1.59am	2.00am to 4.44am	4.45am to 7.14am
01 to 11 Jan	10.45pm to 1.29am	1.30am to 4.14am	4.15am to 6.44am
12 to 20 Jan	10.15pm to 12.59am	1.00am to 3.44am	5.45am to 6.14am
AQU 21 to 31 Jan	9.30pm to 12.14am	12.15am to 2.59am	3.00am to 5.29am
01 to 10 Feb	9.00pm to 11.44pm	11.45pm to 2.29am	2.30am to 4.59am
11 to 18 Feb	8.15pm to 10.59pm	11.00pm to 1.44am	1.45am to 4.14am
PIS 19 to end Feb	7.30pm to 10.14pm	10.15pm to 12.59am	1.00am to 3.29am
01 to 10 Mar	7.15pm to 9.59pm	10.00pm to 12.44am	12.45am to 3.14am
11 to 20 Mar	6.30pm to 9.14pm	9.15pm to 11.59pm	12.00am to 2.29am

Birthdate	Capricorn	Aquarius	Pisces
ARI 21 to 31 Mar	1.30am to 3.14am	3.15am to 4.29am	4.30am to 5.29am
01 to 10 Apr	1.00am to 2.44am	2.45am to 3.59am	4.00am to 4.59am
11 to 20 Apr	12.15am to 1.59am	2.00am to 3.14am	3.15am to 4.14am
TAU 21 to 30 Apr	11.30pm to 1.14am	1.15am to 2.29am	2.30am to 3.29am
01 to 10 May	11.00pm to 12.44am	12.45am to 1.59am	2.00am to 2.59am
11 to 21 May	10.30pm to 12.14am	12.15am to 1.29am	1.30am to 2.29am
GEM 22 to 31 May	10.00pm to 11.44pm	11.45pm to 12.59am	1.00am to 1.59am
01 to 10 Jun	9.30pm to 11.14pm	11.15pm to 12.29am	12.30am to 1.29am
11 to 21 Jun	8.45pm to 10.29pm	10.30pm to 11.44pm	11.45pm to 12.44am
CAN 22 to 30 Jun	8.00pm to 9.44pm	9.45pm to 10.59pm	11.00pm to 11.59pm
01 to 11 Jul	7.30pm to 9.14pm	9.15pm to 10.29pm	10.30pm to 11.29pm
12 to 22 Jul	7.00pm to 8.44pm	8.45pm to 9.59pm	10.00pm to 10.59pm
LEO 23 to 31 Jul	5.45pm to 7.29pm	7.30pm to 8.44pm	8.45pm to 9.44pm
01 to 11 Aug	5.15pm to 6.59pm	7.00pm to 8.14pm	8.15pm to 9.14pm
12 to 23 Aug	4.30pm to 6.14pm	6.15pm to 7.29pm	7.30pm to 8.29pm
VIR 24 to 31 Aug	3.30pm to 5.14pm	5.15pm to 6.29pm	6.30pm to 7.29pm
01 to 11 Sep	3.00pm to 4.44pm	4.45pm to 5.59pm	6.00pm to 6.59pm
12 to 22 Sep	2.15pm to 3.59pm	4.00pm to 5.14pm	5.15pm to 6.14pm
LIB 23 to 30 Sep	1.30pm to 3.14pm	3.15pm to 4.29pm	4.30pm to 5.29pm
01 to 11 Oct	1.00pm to 2.44pm	2.45pm to 3.59pm	4.00pm to 4.59pm
12 to 23 Oct	12.15pm to 1.59pm	2.00pm to 3.14pm	3.15pm to 4.14pm
SCO 24 to 31 Oct	11.30am to 1.14pm	1.15pm to 2.29pm	2.30pm to 3.29pm
01 to 11 Nov	00.45am to 12.29pm	12.30pm to 1.44pm	1.45pm to 2.44pm
12 to 22 Nov	10.15am to 11.59am	12.00pm to 1.14pm	1.15pm to 2.14pm
SAG 23 to 30 Nov	9.30am to 11.14am	11.15am to 12.29pm	12.30pm to 1.29pm
01 to 11 Dec	8.45am to 10.29am	10.30am to 11.44am	11.45am to 12.44pm
12 to 21 Dec	8.15am to 9.59am	10.00am to 11.14am	11.15am to 12.14pm
CAP 22 to 31 Dec	7.15am to 8.59am	9.00am to 10.14am	10.15am to 11.14am
01 to 11 Jan	6.45am to 8.29am	8.30am to 9.44am	9.45am to 10.44am
12 to 20 Jan	6.15am to 7.59am	8.00am to 9.14am	9.15am to 10.14am
AQU 21 to 31 Jan	5.30am to 7.14am	7.15am to 8.29am	8.30am to 9.29am
01 to 10 Feb	5.00am to 6.44am	6.45am to 7.59am	8.00am to 8.59am
11 to 18 Feb	4.15am to 5.59am	6.00am to 7.14am	7.15am to 8.00am
PIS 19 to end Feb	3.30am to 5.14am	5.15am to 6.29am	6.30am to 7.29am
01 to 10 Mar	3.15am to 4.59am	5.00am to 6.00am	6.15am to 7.14am
11 to 20 Mar	2.30am to 4.14am	4.15am to 5.29am	5.30am to 6.29am

An Example of the Method in Action

☆ Jack was born at 8.35 p.m. BST (British Standard Time) on 31 July 1968.

☆ Deduct one hour for BST and make the birth time 7.35 p.m.

☆ The 31st of July is in the first (uppermost) of the three Leo rows.

☆ The penultimate column shows a birth time of 7.30 p.m. to 8.44 p.m.

☆ The column is headed 'Aquarius', so it shows that Jack has the sign of Aquarius on the ascendant.

☆ Furthermore, we can see that he only just comes inside the limits of this birth time, so this gives him an early degree of Aquarius rising.

An accurate computer reading confirms that Jack's ascendant is 5° Aquarius.

3

The Zodiac

The signs of the zodiac are always listed in the following order, and they change on or about the following dates; you need to check the correct date change for any particular year, by asking an astrologer, checking in an ephemeris or by some other means, such as an Internet search.

	SIGN	DATES
1	Aries	21 Mar – 20 Apr
2	Taurus	21 Apr – 21 May
3	Gemini	22 May – 21 Jun
4	Cancer	22 Jun – 22 Jul
5	Leo	23 Jul – 23 Aug
6	Virgo	24 Aug – 22 Sep
7	Libra	23 Sep – 23 Oct
8	Scorpio	24 Oct – 22 Nov
9	Sagittarius	23 Nov – 21 Dec
10	Capricorn	22 Dec – 20 Jan
11	Aquarius	21 Jan – 18 Feb
12	Pisces	19 Feb – 20 Mar

The odd-numbered signs (Aries, Gemini, Leo, Libra, Sagittarius and Aquarius) are masculine/positive/yang in character. This suggests extroversion, confidence and assertiveness, and the ability to solve problems with courage and enterprise. The even-numbered signs (Taurus, Cancer, Virgo, Scorpio, Capricorn and Pisces) are feminine/negative/yin in character. These suggest introversion, shyness and passivity, the ability to nurture, conserve and to solve problems by intuitive means.

I've noticed that the feminine signs are more attuned to business than the masculine ones, and that they make by far the best sales people. Why is this? Well, it's only a theory, but to my mind, the masculine signs have traditionally been the soldiers, warriors and the political thinkers and planners, while the feminine signs have traditionally taken care of the tribe's business, the treasury and the financial and physical well being of the group. Feminine sign people have an ability to read the omens and see which way things are moving. Finally, these people are persuasive and they can sell a dream, so they really do make good sales people.

The signs are grouped into the ancient elements of fire, earth, air and water:

ELEMENTS	SIGNS
The fire signs:	Aries, Leo and Sagittarius
The earth signs:	Taurus, Virgo and Capricorn
The air signs:	Gemini, Libra and Aquarius
The water signs:	Cancer, Scorpio and Pisces

The signs are also grouped into the ancient qualities of cardinal, fixed and mutable:

QUALITIES	SIGNS
The cardinal signs:	Aries, Cancer, Libra and Capricorn
The fixed signs:	Taurus, Leo, Scorpio and Aquarius
The mutable signs:	Gemini, Virgo, Sagittarius and Pisces

The Fire Signs – Aries, Leo Sagittarius

The key ideas here are of energy, enthusiasm and optimism. These people need to be in the centre of whatever is going on, thoroughly involved and even directing. Fire people take the initiative and throw their enthusiasm, intuition and faith behind any enterprise. They never quite relinquish their childhood and are therefore very much in tune with young people and young ideas.

Fire people are egotistic, headstrong and sometimes arrogant, but they are also generous, warm-hearted and spontaneously kind, preferring to help others wherever possible than taking advantage of them. Fire people get things started; they create activity, but need a back-up team to fill in the details for them. These people are quick to grasp an idea and tackle it with gusto, treating life like a kind of game, complete with the sportsman's sense of fair play. They find it impossible to save for a rainy day, but will invariably find a way to earn money when in trouble. Oddly enough, fire people are often very materialistic, measuring their self-worth by their ability to accumulate money and possessions and by having an expensive lifestyle. These people are quick to anger, but rarely sulk.

When a fire sign is on the ascendant, the outer manner is friendly, uncritical and non-hostile, which makes these people good mixers and excellent public relations executives.

☆ Aries rising gives a well-organised, slightly military bearing, which makes them fit well into any kind of paramilitary or civil service organisation.

☆ Leo rising subjects have a dignified and rather formal manner that inspires confidence.

☆ Sagittarius risers have a cheerful, pleasant and rather witty outer manner that suits all kinds of teaching, training and public speaking situations.

The Earth Signs – Taurus, Virgo, Capricorn

The key ideas here are of practicality and security. Earth is concerned with structure and slow growth, as well as conventional behaviour and concrete results. This element is connected with physical things that can be touched and held and which perform a function. Earth people are sensible; they take their time over everything and tend to finish every task that they start. They are shrewd and careful, usually very good at figure work. They are surprisingly dexterous, so they don't often drop or break anything.

Earth people hate to waste anything and they are careful with their money. However, they are invariably generous to their own families. They need a secure home and a solid financial base; requirements that make them appear materialistic to others. Earthy types like to socialise among small groups of familiar people who appreciate their intelligence and dry sense of humour. They may lack spontaneity and can be too cautious and fussy at times, but they are reliable and capable. It takes time to get to know these folk, as they prefer to hang back in social situations, while in business situations they behave in a rather formal manner. Earth people are suspicious of the motives of others and are extra sensitive to hurt. They are slow to fall in love, but when they do, they will remain loyal and faithful to their partner in the majority of cases.

> When an earth sign is on the ascendant, the outer manner is shy, serious and cautious, but they send out pleasant and tactful signals.

☆ Taurus risers are sociable and they are often musical, creative or artistic.
☆ Virgo risers are shy until they get to know people.
☆ Capricorn risers are friendly and they dress well.

The Air Signs – Gemini, Libra, Aquarius

The key idea here is of communication. Air people are concerned with ideas and theories of all kinds, including education, networks and news. They seek answers to questions and then go on to enlighten other people. The network of their nervous system is always on the alert and sometimes over-stretched. These people may be serious-minded intellectuals who are highly involved with the education system or the media, or they may be chirpy, happy-go-lucky types who pick up their street-wise knowledge from the tabloid newspapers and the local pub. They can be found arguing, exploring ideas and becoming excited by means and methods that can apply to anything from the way the universe was formed to a recent football game. They make good journalists, shopkeepers, teachers and travellers, because they are always up-to-date.

Although kind hearted and genuinely concerned with humanity, they can forget their many friends when they are out of sight. They cannot deal with emotional dependency on the part of others, as this drains them, leaving them exhausted and irritable. Air rising subjects love gadgets, especially those that help them communicate or travel, such as computers, fancy telephones and a good fast car.

When an air sign is on the ascendant, the subject is friendly and sociable, but also independent and somewhat detached.

☆ The Gemini riser is constantly busy, but always ready to chat.
☆ The Libra riser is good-looking and pleasant company.
☆ The Aquarian riser can be very friendly or very hostile.

The Water Signs – Cancer, Scorpio, Pisces

The key ideas here are of emotion, intuition and feeling. These people may spend their lives helping others, or at least involving themselves in human problems. They are attached to the kind of matters that bring beginnings, endings and transformations to the lives of others. Watery people respond slowly when asked a question and may appear slow to grasp a new concept, but this is deceptive, because they are filtering the ideas through their layers of intuition before accepting them. Being slow to change, they prefer familiar surroundings and the closeness of family and friends.

Water people are often quite tense and they can worry themselves into illness. They need a lot of understanding, as their moods and emotions make them changeable and unfathomable at times. They are the kindest of friends, often giving practical and sensible help when it's needed, but they cannot take too much neurotic dependence from others. These people are hypersensitive, creative and often psychic. They can appear withdrawn and distant in some cases, but they desperately need stable relationships with plenty of love and affection.

> When a water sign is on the ascendant the subject will hide his true feelings. He fears the world around him; he feels a strong need to protect himself, and also in some cases, to protect the helpless. What you see is definitely not what you get with these people.

☆ Cancerians appear chatty and helpful and they do well in any situation that requires tact.

☆ Scorpio risers use many different forms of camouflage, one of their favourites being offensiveness and an off-putting manner. It's always worth being patient with such people, because there is often a reason for their difficult attitude, and the reward is usually worth the effort.

☆ Pisces risers may appear soft and gentle or abrupt and offensive, depending upon their choice of camouflage. The signals they give out are consciously or subconsciously chosen for their effect, making them appear fierce, friendly, peaceful or docile depending upon their choice of mask.

Cardinal Signs – Aries, Cancer, Libra, Capricorn

Cardinal people cannot be held under anyone's thumb, they need to take charge of their own world. Their energies may be directed towards themselves, their homes and families or to the wider world of work and politics. The cardinal signs, being on the angles of a birthchart, provide the energy and initiative to get things moving.

Fixed Signs – Taurus, Leo, Scorpio, Aquarius

Fixed people have the strength and endurance to see things through and to uphold the status quo. They rarely change their homes, careers or partnerships, preferring to live with an existing situation rather than face uncertainty. Fixed people are loyal and dependable, but also very obstinate. They project an image of strength that is an effective shield for their considerable vulnerability.

Mutable Signs – Gemini, Virgo, Sagittarius, Pisces

These people can adapt to the prevailing circumstances at any given time while, at the same time, managing to alter a situation to suit themselves. Mutable people can steer projects through periods of transition as well as bringing things to a conclusion. They work in fields where things, jobs or people pass through their hands and then come to an end or leave to go on their way. Although gentle and likable, mutable people can be ruthless when the need arises.

4

Aries

Ruled by Mars

The whole art of war consists of getting at what is on the other side of the hill.

Arthur Wellesley, 1st Duke of Wellington

Aries is a cardinal sign, so it likes its own way and it's also a fire sign, which implies enthusiasm and impulsiveness. It's masculine/positive in its approach, which suggests an outwardly extrovert nature. Aries rising is a sign of short ascension, which means that it only applies in the northern hemisphere for a very short period of time in any day, making these people rather thin on the ground.

Early Experiences
Many Aries rising children are born into military families who move about from one place to another. They may also spend a part of each year at boarding school, so the child experiences feelings of strangeness, dislocation and of distance from family and familiar surroundings. Self-reliance and some measure of self-centredness are natural for Aries risers, even if their childhood experiences don't force this upon them, and this can make it difficult for them to form successful family relationships later on. The Aries riser may opt for a life in the services, where he becomes part of a larger family-type group. Several years ago, I did a horoscope for a middle-aged lady who was coming to the end of a service career. She told me that it had been a good life full of travel and fellowship, and that she wasn't quite sure what she was going to do with her time now that she was becoming a civilian.

Aries risers who grow up in a normal, stay-at-home family, often experience discord and conflict. There may be a difficult relationship between the child and his parents, and this is especially true of the father/son relationship. There can't be two bosses in one family, and in this case, neither wants to concede any kind of authority to the other. It's quite usual for the two to be very different in character with little real understanding between them; so, it seems that neither can really approve of the other and there could be some noisy disagreements.

It's worth remembering that an Aries rising nature makes for a noisy, bouncy and rather bumptious child whose restless behaviour and argumentative ways can aggravate even the most saintly of parents. In some cases, the parents are sporty and adventurous, and they encourage a kind of gung-ho bravery in the child. This is all very well if the child is also an outdoor and athletic type, but it isn't so great otherwise.

Women who have this rising sign may not fall into the traditional feminine role. This does not imply that all Aries rising women are gay, or that they are militant feminists. On the contrary, these women get on very well with men, enjoying their company and sharing their interests. Some women prefer not to marry, either living an independent life with or without boyfriends or finding happiness within a career. Those who do marry and have a family need an interesting career outside the home in order to sop up their extra energy and give them something worthwhile to do. Fortunately, these days, there is plenty of scope for the sporty, extrovert, enthusiastic Aries rising woman to have the unrestricted, independent kind of lifestyle that she needs.

The IC is concerned with family matters, and your IC is in probably in the family-minded sign of Cancer. This makes you a surprisingly caring family member, even to the extent of sacrificing a great deal for your loved ones.

Many Aries rising people come from small families and there may be little contact with relatives. The Aries rising child, therefore, doesn't have the opportunity of benefiting from a wider family group, and this leaves him with only his parents' views and values to fall back on. Frequently, these values are distorted and lacking in common sense. Furthermore, the Aries riser is often an only child, or so separated in age and type from the other siblings that he feels like an only child.

It's likely that one or both parents disliked you or saw no value in you. There was no discernible reason for this; you were simply viewed as an irritation or an inconvenience. This leads many of you to seek self-validation through marriage, often marrying young and choosing an older partner, or someone who is deemed wiser and more competent at the game of life. If the marriage doesn't work out, you may begin to philander. There is no guarantee that second or subsequent relationships work out either, unless you are able to go through a good deal of self-analysis and reach a stage where you can finally throw off the distorted lessons of your childhood.

Some Aries rising people succeed in one-to-one relationships, but then face difficulties in relating to their children, either leaning too far towards the position of authority and dominance, or overdoing the nurturing role by clinging to them and sacrificing on their behalf for far too long. All Aries rising subjects have the sign of Capricorn on their midheaven, and it seems as if top of the chart (Capricorn) leads to too much authority, while the bottom of the chart (Cancer) leads to too much clinging.

However, nothing stays the same forever; children grow up and relationships come and go. With a bit of luck, you can learn from life. Perhaps in compensation, Aries rising subjects often make lots of good friends, while others make a viable family out of a couple of pet animals.

Basically, this is neither the best nor the worst sign to have on the ascendant. There may have been loneliness in childhood, but this seems to breed self-reliance and doesn't usually cause you to have any difficulty in relating to others later on in life. Aries rising is a sociable sign and on the whole, a cheerful and optimistic one.

Appearance

Remember to make allowances for racial differences, family tendencies and the influence of the rest of your birthchart when looking at astrological appearances.

The Aries influence would suggest a medium to small stature with a strong and muscular body that may run to fat later. Your arms and shoulders are strong and you can lift and carry surprisingly heavy weights for your size. Your face is broad across the eyes and may be rounded with a rather large head for your body. Aries rising eyes are neither protruding nor deep set, they stare out honestly from under thick, arched eyebrows.

Aries rising women can do a lot with eye make-up, as there is a rather large and flat area of eyelid to play with. The hair may be reddish in colour, quickly going grey. Men of this sign lean towards baldness - well, they do say that bald men are sexy! Women may moan about their hair or dislike their round faces.

Outer Manner

You present yourself in a cheerful, friendly, non-hostile manner, but may find it hard to conceal your contempt for those whose minds and actions are slower than your own. Not being easily influenced, you prefer to make up your own mind about everything, and you can appear rather opinionated. Others see you as quick, clever and courageous, but they may become annoyed by your tendency to push yourself to the front of every queue and to fight for the best of whatever is going. Your sense of humour and child-like appeal can help you get away with murder - especially with the opposite sex.

The Midheaven

The midheaven shows the subject's aims and ambitions, his public standing and his attitude to work outside the home. It can often throw light on strange or unexpected behaviour in a way that even the Sun, Moon and Ascendant don't always address. Some rising signs usually have only one possible MC, while others can have two or even three possible MCs, depending on the time of year in which a person was born, along with the hemisphere and latitude of birth.

In the northern hemisphere, Aries rising can only have a Capricorn MC, but in the southern hemisphere, it is just possible for those born with very late Aries rising to have an Aquarian MC.

The MC also shows the type of person whom you find attractive, so someone whose sun sign was the same as your MC could make you very happy.

Aries/Capricorn

Despite not showing much interest in studying while young, you may return to study later in order to gain some specific qualification, because you have more ambition than is immediately obvious to outsiders.

This MC suggests that you work best in a well-ordered structure, perhaps in a large public service organisation. Some of you prefer to run your own well-planned businesses. You are determined and capable. Your leadership qualities and common sense attitude to money can lead to great success, but this could well come rather late in life. You prefer to start something new, but if you do take over an existing position or an existing team, you soon reorganise it to reflect your own personal style.

You could be drawn to the Arian careers of engineering, building, public service or the armed services, or to the Capricorn ones of business and banking. You may be interested in national or local politics as a career. Your brain is excellent and, if the rest of the chart backs this up, you could find a future in the academic world but you also like to work in an area that helps the public or that improves the environment. You may spend several years coasting along in a job until a change of circumstances propels you towards success.

Aries/Aquarius
This rare combination adds idealism to the personality and it makes you far more interested in the future than in the past. This Asc/MC combo can give you truly inspired ideas and great intuition, so you may become a wonderful inventor or a revolutionary - even to the point of becoming an icon in of the Che Guevara type. However, this combination is not good for practicality or even for basic common sense in some cases. You really must try to keep your feet on the ground and avoid getting so hung up about something that you become a bore or you will lose that great gift of sociability and popularity that is such a large part of your success.

The Descendant
When Aries is rising, the descendant is Libra. The fiery, enthusiastic Aries is attracted by the calm detachment of Libra, including this sign's pleasantness, good taste and desire for harmony and balance. Librans are often good looking and stylish too, but Librans like to argue and once they start, they don't know when to stop.

Love and Relating
Your most attractive features are generosity, honesty, spontaneous kindness and a sense of humour. To be honest, as long as your partner is humourous, intelligent and tolerant of your daft behaviour, you will be happy and so will your partner. You need an independent partner who has work and interests of his or her own, or better still, someone who doesn't need to be waited on hand and foot. However, you need them within phone-shot so that you can have your needs attended to immediately! Aries risers don't require a terribly domesticated partner, but you do need

help in the house and with the children, as you are not especially domesticated or tidy yourself.

Your partner must give you space, not only for your career, but also for your hobbies and interests. You need to be able to take off from time to time, either on business trips or sporting holidays with a group of mates. Your partner must understand that there is a side of you that needs this kind of freedom, and that this doesn't constitute either a lack of loyalty or a dereliction of duty.

You love your children very deeply, and want the best for them, often going to great lengths to educate them. Try not to dominate your children or to show impatience, especially if they seem slow, timid, introverted or clumsy. If you behave impatiently to this kind of child, he will freeze up, making him even more awkward and withdrawn, and will subsequently deprive you of the special kind of warmth that you could have from a loving parent/child relationship.

With your abundance of energy, sex is an obvious necessity, and even a slightly dodgy relationship will work for you if the sexual side is good. In some ways, you suit a moody, changeable partner who varies in his or her sexual needs and responses from one day to the next, so that you can avoid your pet hate - boredom.

Health

Traditionally, Aries rules the head down as far as the upper jaw. Therefore, headaches, eyes, ears, sinuses and the upper teeth are trouble spots. Some Aries rising subjects suffer from acne well into adult life. You have neither the time nor the nature to give in to illness, but sudden fevers and accidents are possibilities. You can become quite ill at times, but will bounce back quickly, because your resistance is generally high. You enjoy food and may be a drinker, therefore weight gain could present a problem later in life. However, if you maintain your preference for an active life, you quickly use up the extra calories. Arian skin is often very pale and delicate, so you have to put on plenty of sunscreen, and even cover up on very sunny days.

Additional Information
☆ You may have a quiet voice, and possibly a slightly high one.
☆ Some of you love animals, and you may particularly enjoy horse riding.
☆ You may also like travel, hunting of various kinds and chasing after any kind of dream.

☆ You spend freely on clothes, although you don't always look after them properly.

☆ You can be a strange host, as you like to ensure that your visitor is sitting comfortably with a drink and a biscuit, and then just as they think they are in for a good old gossip, you wander off and find something to do somewhere else in the house.

☆ Some of you have problems with parents and partners who drink or use drugs.

☆ You will probably have a lifelong interest in sports, both as a spectator and as a participant. You particularly like team sports and anything to do with speed.

Aries Rising Celebrities

John Lennon
Joe Cocker
Billy Graham
Bette Midler
Joan Baez
Martina Navratilova

5

Taurus

Ruled by Venus

Shall I compare thee to a summer's day?
Thou art more lovely and more temperate:
Rough winds do shake the darling buds of May,
And summer's lease hath all too short a date.
William Shakespeare, Sonnet

Taurus is a fixed sign, which means that Taureans like to stay with a situation and see it through. It's also an earth sign, which implies practicality and a stubborn nature. It's feminine/negative, which suggests introversion. This is a sign of short ascension in the northern hemisphere, so only a few people are born each day with this ascendant. However, it's not quite as short as Pisces or Aries, so there are a few more of you around than there are of the latter.

Early Experiences
Taurus rising suggests comfort, and this was certainly true of your childhood. All the earth signs place an emphasis on the need for material security and, in the case of any earth sign on the ascendant, the parents may accumulate money and goods in reaction to their own experiences of childhood poverty. They probably had to work very hard in order to make a home and bring up children. By the time you came along, your parents may have got over the early struggles, or may have still been trying to get it all together. Either way, the message given to the Taurus rising child is one of the need for security, comfort and, better still, wealth.

The old-fashioned virtues of a steady job, money in the bank and solid family life were programmed into you, but it's also possible that values of crass materialism and the devil-take-the-hindmost could also have been pushed upon you. This is fine if you have the same kind of requirements elsewhere in your birthchart, but not so good if you have a gamut of planets in a completely different type of sign. Another and far more serious problem is that, although you were taken care of materially, you may have suffered emotional deprivation. One person with Taurus rising that I know had a mother who suffered badly from depression, which made her unavailable to the child.

When a rising sign is both earthy and fixed, there is a strong possibility that one or both of the parents behaved in an authoritarian manner. Approval may have been given and withheld in subtle ways, making you withdrawn and rather mulish in return. Another possibility is that your father was a slightly awesome figure. However, there is much that's good about this rising sign, and one could do a lot worse than to be born with a Taurean ascendant.

Your parents' outlook was conservative and their behaviour expressed moderation, commonsense, practicality and kindness. You were encouraged to be kind, thoughtful and conscientious. In the unlikely event that you grew up in anything other than the nuclear family, this would have been because one of your parents died. You are unlikely to have witnessed open discord or divorce at first hand. Civilised, unexpressed discontent might have been the order of the day in your parent's household.

You may have grown up with parents who were wrapped up in one another, leaving you emotionally stranded, so that you learned to demand nothing and to avoid bringing the familiar look of irritation to their faces. If you were lucky enough to find another relative or perhaps a person outside the family to whom you could relate, the situation would not have been quite so bad. You may have been at odds with a brother or sister, either envying them for being more successful and more acceptable to your parents than you were, or on the other hand, you may have despised them for being dull, incompetent and irritating. This situation would also have caused you to hide your real feelings, to become devious or to boil inwardly. On occasions, your rage would be towering, frightening and quite destructive. As you grew older, you managed to avoid scenes and ignore unpleasantness, but when pushed, you might erupt in anger or retreat into a world of silent withdrawal that's incomprehensible to others.

Many of you love gardening, because you can enjoy both the scent and beauty of the flowers and growing good things to eat. It's possible that your parents were farmers or landscape gardeners, because there is a natural feeling for the land and all that it produces. The twin messages of conservatism and conservation would lead you to create and to build rather than destroy, and to continue rather than to bring things to a close.

Your family may have been instrumental in introducing you to the world of music, dance or art. You have a natural appreciation of beauty and harmony, so you would have enjoyed these things. If your home life was stable and your parents loving, united and caring, the situation at school may have been a problem. You were not the kind of child to cause trouble at school, and disruption and disobedience is hardly your way of doing things. Nevertheless, unless the rest of the chart is an intellectual one, you were probably slow to catch on, especially in the years before adolescence.

If your parents and teachers accepted you as you were without trying to get you to perform miracles, your school life would have been pleasant, if rather unproductive. However, your teachers may have made you feel worthless and a failure. Worse still, Taurus risers are not the sportiest of children. Many are plump and they all hate to feel cold, wet and uncomfortable. Neither you nor your parents could see any value in romping around on a muddy sports field, although a Sunday afternoon tramp across the field with a dog was quite another matter. Your natural talent and interests lay in the areas of art and music. Nowadays, these interests are fostered for both sexes, but in the days when boys had to be boys and self-expression was not on the curriculum, this could have caused some suffering.

You probably enjoyed working with natural substances such as wood or clay, and you like to cook nice food. Many Taurus rising subjects develop an interest in reading, maths and finance, and they go on to educate themselves later in life at their own pace.

Appearance
Remember to make allowances for racial differences, family tendencies and the influence of the rest of your birthchart when looking at astrological appearances.

Taurus rising women look luscious when young, but have to guard against weight gain later in life. Your complexion is clear, your eyes are marvellous and, in white races, your skin is rather pale and luminous. Your pleasant smile and gentle manner add to your attractive looks. It's fairly common for members of this rising sign to have a 'Churchillian' appearance around the mouth.

Outer Manner

Your outer manner is pleasant and slightly reserved, but friendly and non-hostile. You enjoy a chat with neighbours or colleagues from the office, you probably enjoy listening to office gossip and jokes. You have a good clean sense of humour that doesn't depend upon cruelty or sarcasm for effect. You appear slow moving to others, preferring to make your way through life at quite a gentle pace. Some Taurus risers give an appearance of hardness, especially in business situations.

The Midheaven

The midheaven shows the subject's aims and ambitions, his public standing and his attitude to work outside the home. It can often throw light on strange or unexpected behaviour in a way that even the Sun, Moon and Ascendant don't always address. Some rising signs usually have only one possible MC, while others can have two or even three possible MCs, depending on the time of year in which a person was born, along with the hemisphere and latitude of birth.

In the case of births in the UK and in similar (northern) latitudes, the Taurus rising midheaven is always in Capricorn. In much of the United States, people who have a late degree of Taurus on the ascendant may have Aquarius on the MC.

Taurus/Capricorn

Capricorn, like Taurus, is an earth sign, but it's cardinal in nature, whereas Taurus is fixed. This cardinality on the MC may be one of the reasons why so many Taurus risers go in for running their own show, by owning their own businesses. You produce or supply goods that are practical and useful. You may run a shop, a gardening service, something in the farming or farm-supply line or a small factory. Many of you work in the building trade. Your love of beauty and your subtle sense of touch could lead you into the fields of dressmaking, cooking and craftwork. Some of you take up beauty therapy or become involved with the cosmetic industry, possibly as make-up artists. Many others find their way into the entertainment world, often as singers. However, life being what it is, many Taurus rising people actually work in offices and banks.

The Capricorn connection gives a fondness for big business and banking, while the Taurean thoroughness ensures that errors are few.

Taurus/Aquarius
Generally speaking, Taurus rising subjects resist pressure and dislike hectic or worrying jobs, but the Taurus/Aquarius combination is a little more able to cope with this. Remember that these are both fixed signs that need to do things at their own pace and do them in their own way. The ingenuity of Aquarius could produce a competent wheeler-dealer or someone who reaches the top in an unusual career. The combination of these two could produce a show-business impresario, the owner of a respected art gallery or auction house, or a top editor. This combination adds determination and stubbornness.

Despite the fact that the midheaven is supposed to represent one's direction in life, it can also show the type of person who might attract you, especially if you require a partner who is in sympathy with your goals. Therefore, a partner who has a strong Capricorn or Aquarius emphasis on the chart could appeal to you.

The Descendant
Your descendant is in Scorpio, so you are attracted to strong, determined people. You seem to be looking for the fireworks that accompany the Scorpio, either in the form of uncertain moods or sexual energy. I have no evidence of a particularly high incidence of Taurus/Scorpio relationships, but I think that this combination would work quite well. Both partners need stability in relationships, both are happier in familiar surroundings than with a life of constant change, and both are dutiful family members who are also orientated towards getting on in life. There is much in common but there are times when Scorpio's moods might be hard for Taurus to take. Both signs prefer commitment to playing the field.

Love and Relating
You can cope with a financially independent partner or even one who is heavily involved with a career, just as long as the emotional security is there. You need the love that might have been missing during your childhood. You like to know where your partner is, also what they are doing - not because you distrust them, but because you feel safer if there are no mysteries going on around you. You also like your partner to be around at mealtimes.

A couple of female acquaintances of mine who live with Taurus rising men, tell me that they are very well looked after in bed! On a more serious note, what Taurus rising subjects like best and need most are emotional security and a peaceful home. The adult Taurus rising subject may still suffer the residual effects of the childhood lack of closeness and touch.

Health

Taurus is a robust sign with good powers of recovery. The weak spots are the throat, thyroid gland and the lower teeth. You may be prone to diabetes.

Additional Information

☆ If this person finds a partner, he or she never really lets go; for instance, one guy left his wife for another woman, and then had an affair with his wife, eventually returning to her.

☆ Some can be argumentative and hurtful, while others can be very stingy, even over small and inconsequential things. Some don't like to hold hands or be touched.

☆ Some dress in an extremely unconventional style, to the point of looking really weird.

☆ These people rarely drop anything, so they are probably good at catching a ball. They are also very dexterous.

☆ Some are practical and sensible, others are the complete opposite, it seems that there are no half measures with this sign.

☆ Most seem to love cats.

☆ Many have a conventional day job and an absorbing hobby, such as singing or dancing.

☆ Some are religious.

Taurus Rising Celebrities

Dionne Warwick
Amelia Earhart
Mia Farrow
Liza Minelli
George Lucas
Robert Kennedy

6

Gemini

Ruled by Mercury

The flower that smiles today
Tomorrow dies:
All that we wish to stay
Tempts and then flies.
What is this world's delight?
Lightening that mocks the night.
Brief even as bright.
      Percy Bysshe Shelley, Mutability

This sign is mutable, which implies flexibility of mind, and an air sign, which implies an intellectual approach to everything.

It's masculine/positive, which suggests an outwardly extrovert nature.

Early Experiences
If you have this rising sign, your childhood may have been unsatisfactory, emotionally deprived or even something of a horror story; there may even have been a mystery surrounding your origins. If your childhood was genuinely all sweetness and light, I suggest that you actually re-check your birth time! I call this the 'orphan's ascendant', because there is a feeling of being left out in the cold. A surprisingly high proportion of orphans, fostered and adopted children seem to be born with Gemini rising. Many people who started out with two parents in the normal manner seem to mislay one or both of them somewhere along the way! Even if you were brought up in a normal nuclear family, there would have been feelings of isolation and of being a square peg in a round hole. All this would have been bad enough for the silent,

withdrawn type who is given to hiding his feelings and putting on an act of dumb acceptance, but you need to communicate and to connect with other people on an intellectual level. You also like to analyse yourself and the world around you in order to put it into a sensible and meaningful kind of order.

There may have been difficulty in your dealings with brothers and sisters and you may have grown up in a patched-together extended family. If you came from a large family, you may have missed out in the rush to gain your parent's attention, or you may be so different from your natural parents and siblings that you appear to have originated from a different planet. You were probably one of the younger children, or even actually the youngest child in the family, born to parents for whom the novelty of parenthood had rather worn off. Older siblings may have pushed you around, and your parents might have ignored you or left with minders, while your mother went out to earn much-needed extra money. Something may have gone badly wrong early in your childhood, maybe the death of a parent or some kind of financial disaster. You may have been acutely aware that the people with whom you had been left, looked after you under sufferance or for money. Even in a more normal family, there is a feeling of being the odd one out. You may have been an academic child in a practical family, or a school failure in a family where the only things that counted were brains and exam papers. You may have had a personal or religious outlook that was different from that of the rest of the family.

If your childhood was actually quite tolerable, you will have gained from the better side of this ascendant. The benefits are exposure to books, ideas and teaching aids of one kind or another from an early age. You were encouraged to read, write and to express yourself. If self-expression in the form of too much talking was discouraged, you will have been encouraged by your teachers to write, draw and make things. Being restless and lively, you enjoyed sports or dancing and you could have achieved a high standard. It's possible that you enjoyed being involved in some kind of youth organisation, but probably not for long, as you hate to be regimented. Even as an adult, you enjoy movement and often do most of your thinking while walking or exercising in the local swimming pool. Gemini risers have an inventive streak and are often dexterous, so you can always find something to do. You like animals and pets, as they love you without judging you. You probably talk to the goldfish, which is just one manifestation of your marvellous communications skills.

You are surprisingly ambitious and there is a feeling that, if you can develop a level of strength, power and self-esteem, you can avoid being laughed at and shoved out of the way. There are some among you who go through a sticky marriage or two before you realise that you have a right to be loved and to be treated decently. Gemini rising people are workers, and this is your salvation. You probably have two or more careers going at once, together with a couple of committee positions to boot. You need to feel important and one day, you realise with a jolt that you *are* important and no one talks down to you any more. The Gemini rising clown disappears then, being replaced by the Gemini rising ringmaster.

Appearance

Remember to make allowances for racial differences, family tendencies and the influence of the rest of your birthchart when looking at astrological appearances.

You may have pretty awful problems with your teeth, requiring years of wire braces or even operations to alter the shape of your jaws. Your hair may be fine and in need of a lot of attention. Your hands and feet are neat, and you try to maintain a rather stylish and youthful appearance throughout life. Your chic, attractive clothes reflect your busy super-modern lifestyle. Your car is an important part of your turnout, and this is small, neat, sporty and fast.

Outer Manner

Your outer manner is cheerful, confident and friendly. Some of you can be offensive and upsetting at times, but your sharp-edged cleverness is a shield that protects your vulnerability and shaky sense of self-esteem. You can appear strong, efficient and businesslike, but if you feel threatened in any way, you can be cutting and hurtful. Females with this sign on the ascendant give an appearance of capability and efficiency that doesn't seem to detract from their femininity. The Gemini rising mind is masculine and the mental processes are logical and orderly, more suited to the engineer or computer programmer than anyone's idea of a dizzy woman.

You use your hands while talking and may be emphatic when excited about something. You remain young looking throughout life. You may actually fear old age, but your attitude and appearance guarantee that you remain youthful, even when old. Your quick mind and sense of humour are delightful. Your friendly, non-hostile manner wins you many friends.

The Midheaven

The midheaven shows the subject's aims and ambitions, his public standing and his attitude to work outside the home. It can often throw light on strange or unexpected behaviour in a way that even the Sun, Moon and Ascendant don't always address. Some rising signs usually have only one possible MC, while others can have two or even three possible MCs, depending on the time of year in which a person was born, along with the hemisphere and latitude of birth.

It's possible for those who were born in southern areas of Europe or the USA to have Capricorn on the MC, but for British births, the MC will be Aquarius.

Gemini/Capricorn

Those of you who have Capricorn on the MC are ambitious and determined, looking for security and advancement. You can put your mind to the job and get on with it in a way that other people can only envy. You can turn your communicating skills to good account by sticking at a job and climbing slowly up the career ladder. The earth sign quality of Capricorn suggests that you are probably attracted to work where the values are material, such as in business, banking and large corporations, because you feel a need to achieve something solid by your efforts. This combination could make you a highly skilled and ambitious operator. Alternatively, you could find a comfortable job and stick with it for years without going any higher, as long as there were plenty of new faces around for company and entertainment.

Gemini/Aquarius

The vast majority of Gemini rising subjects, however, have Aquarius on the mid-heaven and this brings both vision and humanitarianism into the picture. A measure of idealism in your choice of career, coupled with your need to communicate, leads you towards the whole area of teaching and training others. If you follow any of the other typically Gemini careers, such as sales representative, journalist, writer, broadcaster or telephonist, you will still try to help people, both on a personal day-to-day basis or by means of communicating useful or instructive ideas.

Gemini's ruling planet is Mercury. In mythology, the Roman god, Mercury, was a messenger who worked for all the gods, but especially for Apollo. Indeed, he was Apollo's errand-boy and he did a good deal of his boss's dirty work, often getting the blame for it, which is a familiar situation, even today!

Another, more satisfying side of this god's work was healing, and this still draws Mercurial people even now. Strictly speaking, the healing attributes are often laid at the feet of the other Mercury-ruled sign of Virgo, but Geminians do their bit in their own way. The idealistic Aquarian midheaven coupled with the Gemini need to help can lead to a medical or nursing career, although the need to communicate often manifests itself in some kind of counselling work. Therefore, psychiatry, marriage guidance or the counselling side of astrology could appeal to you, either as a full-time occupation or as a satisfying sideline.

The presence of such forward looking air signs on both the ascendant and mid-heaven gives an interest in information technology and communications, both from an engineering point of view and by working directly in the broadcasting field. Some Gemini rising subjects become Tarot readers or spiritual healers.

The MC can throw some light on the kind of partners you choose, both in business and in personal life. You may be attracted to people who reflect the values of the sign on your midheaven.

The Descendant

When Gemini is rising, the descendant is in Sagittarius. In theory, you should find yourself especially attracted to Sagittarians. In practice, you could be attracted to any one of the 12 signs – or none of them! Perhaps you look for Sagittarian values in your friends. The Sagittarian values are intelligence, broadmindedness and a taste for adventure.

If your ascendant is late in Gemini, much of your seventh house will be in Capricorn, which will encourage you to seek out a reliable and responsible kind of partner, perhaps one who is in a position of power and influence.

Love and Relating

This is above all a sign of the intellect, so a stimulating partner is a necessity. You can even put up with an absolute rat more easily than you can a boring partner. It hardly needs to be stressed that the old familiar triangle of 'safe partner and thrilling but unreliable lover' could have been made for you. Even a thrilling but unreliable partner is all right, just as long as you can still enjoy your first real loves, which are your work and your hobbies!

Gemini risers are curious, so you probably experimented with sex quite early in life and there is an element of the 'don't die wondering' syndrome here. To be honest, you can live without sex, as long as you are creatively occupied, but your need for comfort and company will soon draw you back to companionship. Your greatest need is to communicate, so you are bound to take the needs of a partner into account.

Health

Gemini rules the arms, shoulders, wrists and hands, also the bronchial tubes and lungs. Therefore, asthma, bronchitis and rheumatism are all possible complaints. Strained ligaments and broken wrists are common, too. Your nerves are delicate, so you could expect skin eruptions, allergies, migraine and nervous bowel problems. You may have an occasional spell of hysteria due to overstretched nerves, or as a result of too much worry. If ever a sign benefited from meditation, massage and relaxation techniques, this is the one.

Additional Information

☆ People with this sign rising are clever. They have quick minds and an aptitude for studying and for modern working methods. Some make good teachers.

☆ All are good with words, either as politicians, writers or broadcasters.

☆ I've come across cases where the subject's parents were literally on their deathbeds before apologising to the subject for being so dreadful to them. Yet the Gemini rising child was always extremely good to the parent.

☆ As babies and children, Gemini rising subjects are so quick to develop that they are light years ahead of others around them. This causes jealousy and resentment.

Gemini Rising Celebrities

Charlie Sheen
Gregory Peck
Michelle Pfeiffer
Hillary Clinton
Drew Barrymore
Neil Armstrong

7

Cancer

Ruled by the Moon

Keep the home fires burning, while
Your hearts are yearning,
Though your lads are far away they
Dream of home.
          Lena Guilbert Ford, Keep the Home Fires Burning

Cancer is a feminine/negative sign that belongs to the water group, but we must remember that it's a cardinal sign, which implies strength and determination. Even though Cancer is deemed to be a gentle sign, oriented towards the feminine principles of home and family, people with this sign rising know what they want and won't do without it for long. This is a sign of long ascension; therefore, there are many people with this sign on the ascendant, at least in the northern hemisphere.

Early Experiences
You were probably well cared for by at least one of your parents and never left for long periods with strangers, nor were you badly treated. Very few people have a perfect childhood, and one could argue that a completely trouble-free childhood is a poor training for adult life. It's better if a little rain does fall from time to time, so that one learns to use an umbrella! This sign is especially associated with the mother, mother figure or anybody who took on the nurturing role.

Your childhood home would have been fairly comfortable, with a slight emphasis on materialism. You were a wanted child; possibly the first one born into the family, and you were able to have your parent's exclusive attention for a few years at least. Even though it's likely that you were the eldest child in the family, you stayed young at heart. You have a responsible attitude and a slightly dignified manner. You didn't get into any ridiculous escapades when you were young, and neither did you find it necessary to play the part of the clown. You were quiet and rather cautious, a bit inclined to cling to your parents and reluctant to move on, out into the world. This attitude tends to change later, when the progressed ascendant moves from cautious Cancer into adventurous Leo.

There is some evidence of religious or spiritual messages being handed out by your parents, and these are accepted or rejected later in life, according to your changing views and circumstances. Your parents may have encouraged you to follow in their footsteps, but you weren't pressured into doing so. In all probability, you had a good relationship with your father, but he might have been a slightly remote figure, being wrapped up in his work or personal interests. Some Cancer rising subjects have a sneaking contempt for their fathers, considering them to be weak, but sometimes, the father becomes seriously ill either in a dramatic way which frightens the child, or in a lingering way which requires permanent care and attention. One Cancer rising friend of mine told me that his father had a weak and frequently ulcerated stomach, which meant the father needed to eat very carefully, whilst also being protected from worry. This ensured that the mother was the power in the family, so reinforcing the typical Cancerian respect for the power of the mother. Incidentally, unless there are hard aspects from the planet Saturn to your ascendant, you were probably born very easily.

Many Cancer rising subjects experience some kind of problem in connection with their schooling, especially during the secondary or college phase of their education. This stems more from peer group pressure than actual education problems. You were probably rather slow and lazy when young, as you were more inclined to sit and dream rather than to get down to work. However, the desire to conform and a growing awareness that the road to adult success begins with school achievement, ensures that you catch up later and then leave your classmates behind. This increase of academic speed may bring a jealous and spiteful response from your erstwhile school friends. You don't seem to go through the same kind of rebellious phase as other teenagers, although there is some evidence that the famed Cancer rising attitude of obedience to parental wishes doesn't last forever. A time will come when you quietly but firmly reject your parents' preferences in favour of a career or lifestyle of your own choice. Despite these changes of direction, you tend to remain affectionately close to your parents throughout their lives.

Appearance

Remember to make allowances for racial differences, family tendencies and the influence of the rest of your birthchart when looking at astrological appearances.

Cancer rising subjects are attractive rather than beautiful, with chubby features, full cheeks, lips and a nicely shaped nose. Your chest and rib cage are large and your shoulders and arms well covered. This gives males a slightly top heavy look, while females frequently have an hourglass type of figure. Some are chunky and solid looking rather than chubby, and those types often have quite heavily lined foreheads. In white races, the skin is pale and the hair can range from mid-brown to almost black, and it's usually strong and abundant, with a will of its own. Your height is probably small to average, and you have to watch your weight later in life. Your hands and feet are small and neat. Both sexes like to look neat, clean and well turned out.

Outer Manner

Most Cancer rising subjects get over their early shyness and become outgoing adults, often with a talent for salesmanship and the more pleasant kind of company politics. You prefer to pour oil on troubled waters than to stir up a storm. At work, you always appear to be cheerful and friendly. You may have troubles in your life, but you don't blab about them or ever appear downhearted, but when you get home, you can be moody, miserable, angry, irritable and very hard to live with. You can even totally ignore your partner – sometimes for months on end!

You are a bit shy, being rather modest and retiring in new company. You do not really seek friendship and you are not terribly interested in people outside your immediate family. You hate to look outrageous, or to draw attention to yourself or to make a public fool of yourself. You obey the rules, and are generally very Civilised in your manner. You are good to talk to because you are such a good listener.

The Midheaven

The midheaven shows the subject's aims and ambitions, his public standing and his attitude to work outside the home. It can often throw light on strange or unexpected behaviour in a way that even the Sun,

Moon and Ascendant don't always address. Some rising signs usually have only one possible MC, while others can have two or even three possible MCs, depending on the time of year in which a person was born, along with the hemisphere and latitude of birth.

Cancer/Aquarius

There is some conflict here, because Cancer rising seeks security while Aquarius seeks freedom. In resolving this conflict, you may behave in one way dealing with friends and family and in another when pursuing your worldly ambitions. If the signs are allowed to blend rather than conflict, you could be drawn to one of the caring professions, due to the fact that these are both caring signs. Counselling work is a possibility, as is medicine, veterinary work and, of course, teaching. In business, Cancer rising wants to drive a hard bargain, while Aquarius wants to be friends with the world, but both can be tough in business and both hide their true feelings from others. The intuitive skills of astrology, palmistry, graphology, numerology and the Tarot etc. may appeal to you, possibly enough to make a part-time or full-time living from them. Political activity is a natural for you, so you could be drawn to work in the civil service, local government or you may choose to serve on committees.

Cancer/Pisces

This mixture produces a sentimental person for whom continuity is important. You probably prefer to stay in a job where you feel yourself to be appreciated as part of a successful team. The Pisces element can bring confusion regarding your aims, so you could drift along, hoping for the best rather than reaching for a specific goal. If Neptune (the ruler of Pisces) is well aspected in your chart, career muddles will be less of a problem. The combination does not usually bring any burning ambitions; you just want a happy working life and contentment at home. Some of you prefer to work from home or spend your energies looking after children or animals.

The travel trade may attract you, or you may have to travel in connection with your work. You may have an interest in the medical world, osteopathy, aromatherapy or other complementary therapies. All the Cancer/Pisces people whom I know seem to consult alternative medical practitioners either in addition to, or in place of conventional doctors. You find it quite easy to accept the idea of spiritual healing and psychic or mediumistic work, probably due to your own natural highly developed level of intuition. You have a natural affinity with money and budgeting, therefore finance work (which also requires intuition) and fund raising for a charity are possible interests.

Cancer/Aries

This combination brings together two cardinal signs, so you would be unlikely to blindly follow any course of action that was against your own interests. The charm of the Cancerian ascendant masks your willfulness to some extent. You could make a good politician or diplomat because you appear to be sociable and reasonable, but you are usually able to make your point. If you want to, you can push your way to the top by sheer hard work and by keeping your goals clearly in sight, however some of you can't be bothered to make the effort.

You probably prefer self-employment to being part of a team, and may be interested in a mixture of the rather muscular Aries type of job and the gentler, more domestic, Cancerian type. This could lead you to run a small building concern, or to employ a group of gardening contractors or a battalion of office cleaners. Both Cancer, which is associated with patriotism and history, plus Aries, which has military inclinations, lead to an interest in military matters. This could suggest a career in the services (especially the navy) or part-time involvement with a paramilitary organisation. You might be interested in the Scout movement or something similar. Whatever you choose to do, you won't allow the grass to grow under your feet. Other interests, whether as hobbies or as a career, include cooking, teaching, child-care, engineering, interior design and decorating.

The Descendant

Your descendant is Capricorn, which is a conventional sign, so you look for safe and secure relationships. You are sincere in your dealings with others and you seek the same sincerity from them. You need a practical partner who can stand on his own two feet and who has a sense of personal dignity. You are very caring and dutiful in your attitude to others, even when the relationship is a detached one, such as a close colleague at work. You don't appreciate people whose eccentricities include a lack of personal principles, laziness or stupidity, and you appreciate efficiency. You may be attracted to a partner who is ambitious or outstanding, but you must resist the urge to curb or control them.

I haven't noticed any prevalence of Cancer/Capricorn marriages; however, these two signs have much in common, so this could work quite well. Both signs understand the other's attachment to his or her family. Both parties will look after parents, in-laws and grandparents, in addition to children and stepchildren. The cautious attitude suggested by this descendant makes you slow to get into relationships, and inclined to marry later in life than usual.

Love and Relating

Your caution and shyness mean that you are slow to get off the ground in this area of life, and many of you seem to wait until your thirties before marrying and having children; when you do, your intentions are that you stay married, preferably for life. It's possible that this very sense of commitment is one reason for your hesitancy. Another peculiarity of this rising sign is that you are probably most comfortable with a partner who is quite a bit younger or older than you are. You are protective towards your partner, but you may take this a bit too far, becoming a bit of a mother hen.

Cancer rising is not a notably sexy sign. Typical comments are that an affectionate cuddle is as important as sex, and that sex is part of a larger relationship rather than as an end in itself. You need to love and be loved and to have the love of a family around you, and this includes parents, siblings and children. You adore your own children and can give a great deal of love and affection to other people's children, too. Some Cancer rising women unfortunately seem to lose their fragile sexuality as soon as the babies come along. A Cancerian woman will try to re-activate this side of her life to prevent her man from straying.

Health

Traditionally, the areas that give you trouble are the stomach, breasts and the lower end of the lungs. Many Cancer rising subjects seem to have weak throats, and bronchitis, and many also suffer from rheumatism.

Additional Information

☆ You are shrewd, but wealth may elude you, possibly because you are too lazy to follow through on a good idea, or because you financially support other family members.

☆ Some Cancer rising subjects are very tight-fisted, others are just short of money.

☆ Many of you like to stick to a routine at home and at work, so that circumstances rarely take you by surprise.

☆ You must watch a tendency to be cruel. You may think you are defending yourself against potential attack, but in reality, all you may be doing is hurting others for no reason.

☆ Surprisingly, you are flirtatious and sometimes a little bit outrageous, but you don't mean anything by this behaviour.

Cancer Rising Celebrities

Steven Spielberg
Bill Gates
Ian McShane
Robert De Niro
Michelle Obama
Mae West

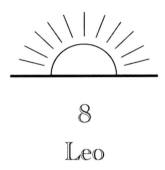

8

Leo

Ruled by the Sun

I suppose that means that I shall have to die beyond my means.
Oscar Wilde - on being presented with a Doctor's bill for an operation towards the end of his life.

Leo is a masculine, positive sign that's fixed in quality; therefore, the subject will present a confident, capable and reliable image to the world. This is a sign of long ascension, which implies that there are a lot of these people about. Oddly enough, we seem to run across far fewer Leo rising subjects in daily life than we do their immediate neighbours of Cancer and Virgo rising. There is no astrological reason for this discrepancy, but there may be some less obvious ones.

Leo rising infants are not strong and they don't all survive the first months of infancy. Secondly, these subjects don't seem to lead ordinary lives; they become captains of industry, sports champions or stars in the entertainment world, which suggests that they are not to be found in the local pub or at the office. Thirdly, this is a royal sign and is actually well represented within the royal family. Even the younger George Bush has Leo rising! Therefore, this sign either carries a pedigree, or thinks it should have one.

Early Experiences
You were a wanted child, but there may have been a problem with your father. He may have been too authoritarian or he may have left the family, or even died. Perhaps someone else came along and pushed you around. I've come across some Leo rising subjects who had success-story fathers who had a very high opinion of themselves, and who made their children

feel inadequate, probably because they saw their children as potential rivals. Some fathers considered their offspring too much like hard work. The relationship with the mother seems to be much easier, although the situation can reverse, with the father being the favourite parent.

In happier households, you would have been encouraged to develop your talents and abilities, but also to conform to set patterns of thought and behaviour. Your parents were traditional in outlook, possibly following some kind of religious belief. Later in life, you question your parents' beliefs and find your own philosophy or religious outlook. You may become interested in spiritual matters, meditation and alternative or complementary medicine.

Your parental home was probably comfortable and your parents fairly well off. They may not have been rich, but they would have been respected in their community. Your parents believed in staying together and working out their problems within the family. Although home life was comfortable and peaceful, you do not seem to have been spoiled or over-indulged. Having said this, I've met one subject whose father died, leaving her mother to find work as a servant at the house of a very wealthy family. Nobody set out to hurt the child, but she couldn't help feeling like a second-class citizen in comparison with the wealthy children around her. There is usually something weird about the childhood when Leo is rising. You would have been told you that you were special in some way, which led to some measure of isolation. Your parents may have favoured you because you were the first child to be born to the family, an only child, or a child of one sex among siblings of the opposite sex. You may have been a much-loved late addition, born when your parents had money to spare, so that your childhood was different to that experienced by your siblings.

Leo rising children are often talented. Many are musical, but some are academic, artistic, creative, dexterous, sporty or mediumistic. A talented child, especially if he comes from a non-talented family, always stands a little apart from others. Whatever has been the cause, the effect is a feeling of being different and of isolation, although this is less noticeable when the rest of the birthchart inclines the child towards good relationships.

Appearance
Remember to make allowances for racial differences, family tendencies and the influence of the rest of your birthchart when looking at astrological appearances.

Leo risers are quite distinctive, so you are probably tall with a slow and regal way of moving. Both sexes are vain and both will go to a lot of trouble to look good. You worry about your hair, which is probably thick, wavy and abundant. Leo men are terrified they might lose their hair, and may spend hours worrying about this. You like to dress fashionably, even glamourously, and to surround yourself with quality goods. A good car is an essential addition to your turnout.

Outer Manner

You are genuinely interested in people and you try to present a kindly, non-hostile personality to the world. Although you can appear arrogant, demanding and unrealistic at times, for the most part, you are liked and admired. Leo rising people have presence, graciousness and inborn public relations skills. You are a good listener and an interesting talker, which makes you popular in social situations. You are quite fussy about your choice of friends, and this is where a touch of the Leo snobbery can often be seen.

The Midheaven

The midheaven shows the subject's aims and ambitions, his public standing and his attitude to work outside the home. It can often throw light on strange or unexpected behaviour in a way that even the Sun, Moon and Ascendant don't always address. Some rising signs usually have only one possible MC, while others can have two or even three possible MCs, depending on the time of year in which a person was born, along with the hemisphere and latitude of birth.

If Leo is rising, you could have either Aries or Taurus on the MC. The Leo/Aries combination adds sparkle to the chart, as both are fire signs. The fixed/fire quality of Leo together with the cardinal/fire quality of Aries make for an ambitious, determined and capable person who attacks his goals with considerable enthusiasm. The Leo/Taurus combination is very fixed, so the individual is less ambitious but more stubborn, determined and practical. All Leo rising people seem to enjoy information technology and most can manage machinery of various kinds.

Leo/Aries

This combination inclines you towards self-employment, management positions and team leadership. Being a faceless member of a team is not really your scene and therefore, even when joining an organisation as a junior member, you stand out from the others and very soon begin to climb up the promotion ladder. You may not appear ambitious in the normal sense of the word, but you seem to drift towards the top, as if it were your rightful place in life. You enjoy success, status symbols and the feeling of being looked up to. Careers that may attract you are engineering, building and the driving of trains, planes and road vehicles. You could be an actor, teacher or jeweller - or a combination of these. You work at a steady pace, but with periods of sheer idleness in between. Needless to say, most of the time, you manage to achieve a great deal. It's possible that you give up the effort at some point, taking early retirement and doing what makes you happy, but you ensure beforehand that you can afford to do this.

Leo/Taurus

This makes for success, just as long as you don't give in to your tendency for laziness. Both signs dislike change and prefer the continuity of a settled job. Both are quite ambitious, even if this is not obvious. You can work at a job purely for the money it brings in, or for the power and influence you might obtain from it; however, you are happiest when your work contains a creative element. Both signs are creative and musical, so you could find work in the fields of fashion, art, music, engineering design, landscape gardening or catering. Your creativity could lead you to start a business of your own or, if you are not career minded, to create a lovely home of your own. If your job doesn't give you an opportunity for creativity, you will look for a creative hobby.

Some people are attracted to those whose Sun sign is the same as their MC sign. This would suggest that the partner is in tune with the subject's aims and ambitions. In your case, you get on well, both at work and in your personal life, with Aries or Taurus people.

The Descendant

When the ascendant is in Leo, the opposite point or descendant is in Aquarius, so you may be attracted to Aquarian qualities in a partner. These qualities are independence; humanitarianism and an individual outlook on life, and you may treat your partners in a slightly Aquarian manner by giving them space. You are incredibly difficult to please, because you choose a partner who is capable, independent and intrinsically fascinating, but then you become uncomfortable and possibly unpleasant because you can't stand the competition.

This Aquarian descendant can cause problems due to the unstable and revolutionary nature of the sign. In terms of relationships, this means that you are likely to be married more than once, and your partners may be rather unusual. In some cases, your partners start out normal and become odd later!

Love and Relating
You want to be loved, but you have to take great care not to destroy a relationship before it even gets off the ground. You are a family person, but you cannot subordinate yourself too far to the wishes of a partner, because you need to be treated with respect. If you feel that your role is important, as either wage earner or homemaker and that your decisions count for something within the home, all is well. The love that you seek takes every form, including the love of your children, genuine care and affection for your mate and of course, sex. Sexually, you are warm, caring, gentle and at the same time, demanding. You have a well-developed sense of touch and you are a generous lover. Any form of ridicule on the part of your partner would spell out the death of the relationship. When things work out well, you can make very successful relationships.

Health
Leo is traditionally associated with the back and the heart, but this rising sign doesn't seem to have an effect on health, so one must look elsewhere on the chart to find the danger points.

Additional Information
☆ Many Leo rising people have golden coloured eyes and a reddish tinge to the hair.
☆ You are very hospitable and a wonderful host, and you can be very kind.
☆ You can also be prey to snobbery, arrogance, a superior attitude and you may be a bully. Try to control such behaviour, as it will ensure that you end up lonely and unhappy once you have driven everyone else away.
☆ You may be fussy about your car, so that you spend a lot of money on it and never allow anyone else to drive it. Alternatively, you may never bother to own a car at all.
☆ You will always feel different in some way, but you enjoy this.

Leo Rising Celebrities

Elton John
Piers Morgan
Edwina Currie
Simon Cowell
Meryl Streep
Tina Turner

9

Virgo

Ruled by Mercury

Men of England wherefore plough
For the lords who lay ye low?
Wherefore weave with toil and care
The rich robes your tyrants wear?
       Percy Bysshe Shelley, Song to the Men of England

This sign is mutable, which implies flexibility of mind, and it's an earth sign, which suggests practicality, while also being feminine/negative in nature, denoting introversion. Virgo rising is a sign of long ascension, which means that there are plenty of you around.

Early Experiences
One of the questions on my research questionnaire asked, 'would you like to have your childhood over again?' All but one of the Virgo rising respondents replied, 'No, definitely not!' The only one who gave a 'yes' answer had her rising sign on the Virgo/Libra cusp, so that the entire first house was actually Libra. This is such a difficult ascendant to be born with that, if your childhood was abnormally happy, I'd suggest that you re-check your birth time!

Your parental home may have been comfortable or downmarket, but whether your family was rich or poor, their attitude to money was probably frugal. This is assuming that you were brought up in a normal nuclear family, but it's possible that you spent time being looked after by other people.

Sometimes the Virgo rising subject has a reasonable relationship with the mother but a difficult one with the father, and in some cases, the father takes delight in tormenting or bullying the Virgo rising child. In other cases, the father loves the child, but the mother cannot see any good in the child and subjects it to a barrage of criticism and disapproval. Not every case is as extreme as this, but there will be some unfair and undeserved ill treatment at the hands of others at home, at school or both.

Your parents were probably dutiful in their attitude towards you, making sure that you had your practical needs catered for. If they did this out of a sense of obligation rather than genuine affection, you would have been aware of this and you may even have felt guilty for putting them to the trouble of looking after you! You were expected to conform to a set of rules and regulations and to be clean and tidy at all times with polished shoes and straight, unwrinkled socks. Your school may also have been over-disciplined with too much emphasis on stuffy rules.

Your parents expected you to do well at school, to behave perfectly and to maintain a position at the top of the class at all times. This constant pressure and the unremitting requirement for you to be perfect at everything (except maybe for those subjects they themselves felt were unnecessary) could have left you rigid with nerves and prey to all kinds of nervous ailments. On the positive side, you had access to books, educational aids and extra-curricular activities. You were encouraged to read and to learn, and you probably got the hang of this quite early on. Some Virgo rising children don't make friends easily, while others make such good friends, that they become a kind of substitute family. Some of you are happiest in your own company or with your pets. You didn't take much interest in any of the contemporary fads and fancies in which the other children were involved.

You have a surprisingly stubborn and uncompromisingly selfish streak that may not be immediately obvious to others. Your survival instincts are strong, endowing you with a knack of appearing to be accommodating while actually pleasing yourself. Some Virgo rising children actually resist love and affection, behaving so oddly and in such an offensive manner that nobody can really take to them.

Some Virgo rising subjects grow up in an overbearing religious atmosphere where the fear of God is added to the fear of what the neighbours might think. (This is especially so when the IC is in Sagittarius.)

Appearance
Remember to make allowances for racial differences, family tendencies and the influence of the rest of your birthchart when looking at astrological appearances.

Virgo rising subjects are good looking as a rule, especially if they are born with a fairly late degree of the sign rising. You are probably a little taller than average, with a long, slim, well-defined face, thin nose and arresting eyes. All this has to be considered alongside racial differences and the influence of the rest of the chart. Typical subjects have a cheery smile and an intelligent sense of humour that shines out of the eyes. Your complexion is pale, even in the summer, because you haven't the patience to waste time lolling around in the sun. You may be a little overweight or even quite thin with a bit of a potbelly, but your above-average height and your good posture allow you to get away with this.

Outer Manner

Your outer manner is polite, formal and a little guarded. You can hang back and be shy on first meeting, especially in new social circumstances, but you soon warm up when you relax. Your mind is very sharp and you can be surprisingly intuitive. You always appear confident and capable, the very image of the perfect purchasing officer, secretary or nurse. Being shy, you may also appear to be a little standoffish on first acquaintance, and you prefer to let others do the talking, while you assess the people and the situation around you. When you're at ease, of course, you can talk the hind legs off a donkey. You are usually very smartly dressed, in an up-to-date manner with stylish and slightly unconventional clothing.

The Midheaven

The midheaven shows the subject's aims and ambitions, his public standing and his attitude to work outside the home. It can often throw light on strange or unexpected behaviour in a way that even the Sun, Moon and Ascendant don't always address. Some rising signs usually have only one possible MC, while others can have two or even three possible MCs, depending on the time of year in which a person was born, along with the hemisphere and latitude of birth.

In the case of Virgo rising in UK latitudes, the mid-heaven covers the latter part of Taurus and a good deal of Gemini. In southern Europe and the United States, you will only have a Taurus midheaven if your ascendant is in the first couple of degrees of Virgo. The vast majority of people born with Virgo rising have the MC in Gemini.

Virgo/Taurus

The effect of having earth signs on both the ascendant and the MC makes you practical, sensible, obstinate and probably rather materialistic, and this need for security leads you to find work in a safe and established trade.

Both Virgo and Taurus are interested in the growth and production of food, therefore you could work as a farmer, market gardener, dietician or cook. The building trade is another possibility, as is work connected with buildings, such as fitting out, furnishing or dealing with property. The insurance business is also possible. Too much change, challenge and excitement would unnerve you, but a steady, ordinary and reasonable job would suit you well. Virgo is concerned with health and healing, but Taurus can't stand blood and mess, so the prevention of illness by diet and exercise might appeal more than dealing directly with sick people. This combination suggests a need for comfort at home and a good standard of living, and you would strive to provide this for yourself and your family. Taurus is associated with music and Virgo with words, so if your birthchart has a creative slant, you could be drawn to music production.

Virgo/Gemini

This is the sign of the competent secretary, media researcher, nurse or teacher. Mercury rules both signs, so you are very interested in all forms of communication, which includes teaching and studying, writing and publishing, journalism or driving. Your mind is active and you need to express yourself, but your shyness suggests that you are happier as a backroom boy or girl than out in front of the public. You might be interested in nutrition, medical research or methods of plant cultivation, or writing about these things.

You look deeply at whatever you are working on rather than taking anything on face value. Your strong desire to help others can lead you into the counselling or medical fields, especially medical research. Communication in the form of travel and transport might attract you, therefore the travel trades and driving or vehicle maintenance could be good careers. Your meticulous and orderly mind could attract you to computer aided design, systems analysis or accountancy. Other possibilities are electrical work or maintenance, electronics, radar, telecommunications or television and video engineering. Any kind of statistical work might appeal, as might research and analysis. Some Virgo rising subjects make very good historians.

The MC can sometimes denote the kind of person who attracts us or with whom we feel comfortable in day-to-day life. Therefore, you might find that you get on well, both at work and in your private life, with Taurus or Gemini types.

The Descendant

When Virgo is rising, the descendant is in Pisces and this may bring difficulties in relationships. You may attract people who are out of the ordinary or even peculiar. It seems as if this descendant is trying to compensate for your down-to-earth attitude to life by throwing a spanner in the works just where you least need one. You may find yourself attached to a partner who drinks, uses drugs or who is mentally unstable. To some extent, it's your desire to help and to reform others that may land you in this pickle. You may fall for someone who looks all right at first, but who is cruel or unable to relate to others. Some of you take on people with disabilities.

On the plus side, you also attract gentle, rather mystical types who want to care for and serve the needs of the family, just as you do. You seek kindness in a partner and will act kindly and charitably towards them in your turn. You can be happy with a partner who is musical, artistic and caring as long as they also pull their weight at work and at home. You can put up with a lot, just as long as your partner is basically decent and honest. You, yourself, can be decent and totally reliable in practical matters, but potentially unfaithful sexually. Here we go again with those Virgo contradictions.

Love and Relating

This area of your life, as you have probably guessed, has all the appearance of a first-class minefield, especially when one looks at the contradictions in your own nature. You are shy, modest, yet you marry or have sex at an early age, possibly due to a need for love and approval. Some Virgo risers trade sex for company, comfort and companionship. Oddly enough, considering the modesty and fastidiousness of this sign, you have a strong, needy and inventive sex-drive that, coupled with your curiosity, can lead you into all kinds of adventures. In short, despite all the repression, guilt and fear of making a fool of yourself, the enjoyment of lunch, love and lust creates a surprising metamorphosis in you.

Oddly enough, for such a responsible and family-minded sign, you are quite likely to be unfaithful in marriage. Possibly the need to experiment, compare and to analyse is at the back of this, or maybe a need for freedom even within a committed relationship. Maybe it's your way of getting back at a repressive partner or coping with a bad marriage. Your quiet, humourous and laid-back manner is charming and attractive, as is your quite genuine desire to please and above all, to communicate.

Health

Your health is probably lousy. If it isn't, then you will suffer from hypochondria! Traditionally, your skin, bowels and nerves are weak spots, but you could have any ailment you desire. Like your Gemini rising cousins, your nerves will let you down; they will plunge you into an illness whenever the going gets tough. Toothache, backache and inexplicable stomach pains are all possibilities, as are chronic ailments of all kinds. Yet, you are strong and able to overcome horrifying ailments in a way that others cannot.

Additional Information

☆ You are your own worst enemy and you are the first to shoot yourself in the foot. Some of you are too self-critical, others are too ready to open your mouths and criticise others. You can be cutting, sarcastic and hurtful – yet also kind and thoughtful when in the mood.

☆ You may have a loud and piercing voice. As a child, you screamed and shouted a lot, which probably got on the nerves of your parents and teachers. Later in life, you may have screaming rows with your partner and you may shout at your children a lot. If you could just curb this one aspect of your personality, you would do yourself a big favour.

☆ You dress well and you tend to look fairly 'cool'.

☆ You make friends easily and keep them for years, and you are popular. This is just as well, as you like to get out and about and be involved in local matters.

☆ You won't start on anything until you are sure that you can do it perfectly and that you are in no danger of attracting criticism. Sadly, this can lead to you doing nothing and achieving nothing.

Virgo Rising Celebrities

Franklin D Roosevelt
Derek Jacobi
Winston Churchill
John Cleese
Oprah Winfrey
Madonna

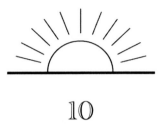

10

Libra

Ruled by Venus

> We don't bother much about dress and
> Manners in England, because as a
> Nation we don't dress well and we've
> No manners.
>
> *George Bernard Shaw, You Never Can Tell*

Libra is a cardinal sign, which means that you like your own way. It's also masculine, positive and airy in character, which suggests an outgoing and enterprising nature. The weird thing is that the ruling planet is Venus, and that causes confusion.

This is a sign of long Ascension, so there are plenty of you around.

Early Experiences
This sign on the ascendant denotes a good start in life, but there can be some drawbacks even when this most pleasant sign is rising. Your parental home was probably comfortable, your parents kind and your relationship with childhood friends reasonable. As a small child, you were good looking, popular and charming and you managed to keep out of any real trouble, both at home and at school. All in all, your childhood experiences were better than most, so what's the problem?

The problem is subtle and it varies a little from one Libra rising subject to the next. Your parents may have left you to your own devices because they were busy. In some cases, the father was a distant figure; he may have travelled away from home in connection with work or he may have walked away from the marriage and left the family. In many cases, he actually died when the subject was very young. Sometimes the relationship with the father is quite good, but the mother nags, ignores the child or makes unreasonable demands. There is not enough respect by the child towards the parents and by the parents towards the child. There may be distance and neglect.

It may be that the subject and his parents have different value systems, or natures that clash, although any clashing will be done quietly when this sign is rising. There are many Libra rising subjects who are lavished with guilt-induced presents by parents who neglect them.

In less difficult circumstances, your parents are good and they understand you, but your sisters and brothers may be less than impressed by your charm, and could have behaved in a jealous and spiteful manner towards you.

You were probably lazy, slow moving, quiet and well behaved. If your parents were not too neglectful, they would have given you every opportunity to stretch your mind and they would have encouraged you to do well at school. It's unlikely that a great deal of pressure was put on you to succeed, but there was pressure to conform and not to make waves.

Being independent, even as a child, it's possible that your religious beliefs and political opinions developed differently from those of your parents. Libra rising subjects don't usually come from a highly religious background, but oddly enough, their parents seem to have strong political views. Belonging as you do to an independent-minded air sign, you would have listened to their opinions and then formed your own at a later stage in life. Although slow to do anything, and very slow to come to any kind of decision, you were quite able to think things out for yourself and to work out what you wanted to believe in.

Even when young, you loved beauty, had taste, and style, and it's unlikely that you grew up in an atmosphere of mess, dirt and disorder. You are not slovenly yourself, and neither were your parents.

You appreciate the arts, music and anything that's attractive and well thought out. You could have been artistically creative, especially if there are other forces on your birthchart to back this up. Libra risers have a natural kind of refinement.

It's possible, even as a small child, that you assisted your parents in planning and working on a garden or in choosing the colour schemes for the house.

Appearance

Remember to make allowances for racial differences, family tendencies and the influence of the rest of your birthchart when looking at astrological appearances.

You are good looking, although not necessarily beautiful. Your features are refined, delicate and attractive. Even if plump, you have a clear skin, beautiful eyes and a lovely smile. In white races, the skin is very fair and the eyes are large, widely set and often a pale luminous grey. You are probably a little below average height with a body which is long in proportion to your legs. Your posture is good and you move with a kind of liquid grace. Your choice of clothing may be conventional or outrageous, but it will always be classy, expensive and in keeping with your personality. You like to keep your clothes for a long time and are prepared to spend money on dry-cleaning.

Outer Manner

You are charm personified. People take to you at once, because of your friendly approach and your genuine interest in what they have to say. Pleasant, humourous and gentle, you are easy to talk to and to get along with, at least on the surface. Your manner of dealing with the world is reasonable, respectful, calm and businesslike; it's rarely brisk or officious. At work you appear to be capable, with an unhurried style that belies your ambition. Friends drift in and out of your life and though you may forget them for a while, you are always pleased to see them again when they reappear. Unfortunately, you may lack sincerity, and intuitive people spot this immediately. In private and to your lovers and work colleagues, you may be extremely confrontational and unpleasant, and you never give an inch in any dispute.

Midheaven

The midheaven shows the subject's aims and ambitions, his public standing and his attitude to work outside the home. It can often throw light on strange or unexpected behaviour in a way that even the Sun, Moon and Ascendant don't always address. Some rising signs usually have only one possible MC, while others can have two or even three possible MCs, depending on the time of year in which a person was born, along with the hemisphere and latitude of birth.

In the UK and Europe, most Libra rising subjects have their midheaven in Cancer. However, those whose ascendant is in the latter part of the sign will have their MC in Leo. For births in the south of Europe and in the United States, almost the whole of this rising sign will have the MC in Cancer and only those with the ascendant in the last few degrees in Libra will have their MC in Leo.

Libra/Cancer

This combination can make for a shrewd businessperson, and you take your time before committing yourself to anything, carefully weighing up the pros and cons. You may be interested in antiques, coin collecting or Egyptology. Libra, being an air sign, is interested in communicating, keeping up-to-date and being out among people, while Cancer likes to work quietly for himself.

This apparent contradiction can be overcome by either doing your own thing inside a large organisation or by doing your own thing in some kind of loose association with others. Cancer, being a caring sign, can suggest a nursing or counselling career, so you may enjoy teaching very young children either in a school or in a Sunday school. This combination is an excellent one for a career in politics, or a quasi-political career such as Trades Union negotiator.

Oddly enough, I've come across a number of electricians and electrical engineers with this rising sign. Maybe the Cancerian MC makes you want to improve people's home and business premises, or maybe it's the presence of air on the ascendant which gives you an affinity to electrical or magnetic forces. Libra is associated with the planet Venus, and this gives you a strong interest in beauty in all its forms, so you may consider working in the field of fashion, cosmetics and design. You may exploit your flair for interior design as a career.

Libra/Leo

This combination suggests a need to leave your mark on the world, and being a big spender, you also need to be a big earner. You may be attracted to a job that offers you a chance to shine or to use your dramatic flair in some way, such as theatrical agent, recruitment consultant or an agony aunt. Both Leo and Libra are creative signs, so you may choose to work in the fields of design, fashion, jewellery, cosmetics or interior design. Your ability to listen and advise could lead you to work as a solicitor, counsellor, consultant, doctor or hypnotherapist. Medical and healing work often appeals to people with this combination. You may have an affinity with Cancer or Leo types, for business or love partnerships.

The Descendant

When Libra is rising, the descendant is in Aries, therefore the enthusiasm and enterprise of Aries types may well attract you. Libra needs a partner who enjoys work, and you are happy to have them work alongside you, as long as they don't try to make your decisions for you. The cardinal quality of the signs on your ascendant and descendant suggest that you must lead, albeit slowly, rather than follow.

You require a fairly calm partner who has a strongly confident centre to his or her personality, because you have a habit of taking your everyday frustrations out on your nearest and dearest, or ignoring them when you're in a bad mood. A clingy, unreasonable or jealous partner is no good for you, as you detest being pinned down or having to account for your movements.

Oddly enough, you succeed in one situation where many others fail, and that's in the area of second marriages, as you don't trouble yourself to argue with step-children or ex-wives or husbands, preferring to keep the peace if at all possible. Inside your own one-to-one relationship, you may be far from peaceful, but to those on the periphery, you appear to be decent and reasonable. If you find yourself drawn into a wider family group, you manage very well, because you enjoy the fun of family life and all the extra opportunities for conversation and advice giving. You like to experiment with relationships, so you may find commitment and faithfulness impossible.

Love and Relating

Despite your cool outer image, relating is never a cool business for you. Somewhere along the line, you will fall in love, and when this happens you will fall hard. You may not show your feelings to the world, but they are strong and deep nevertheless. If you are let down and hurt by this experience, you hide your feelings, but they go down deeper than anyone can guess, and it's unlikely that you will ever allow yourself to be placed in that situation again. This is a shame, because the next person who comes along may be far more worthy of your love, but by then, it's too late. Once you have been burned, you never place your hand in the fire again.

When you do feel intensely about your partner, your lovemaking can reach magical proportions and even when this is not the case, you are a notably good lover. Libra is a hedonistic sign that enjoys any kind of sensual experience, good food and good music and, of course, good sex. You take the trouble to make sure your partner enjoys the experience as much as you yourself, and your sensual laziness ensures that you take your time over the process, and you hate to make love in scruffy surroundings.

Health

Traditionally, the Libran problem areas are the bladder and the soft organs. Your liver and pancreas may be weak, so you should limit your alcohol intake and avoid too much sweet food, as diabetes is a possibility. You could have a weight problem, but your natural vanity will urge you to take action about this. Libra rules the motor development of the nervous system and, therefore, can be involved with rheumatic or nervous problems, particularly in the spinal column.

Additional Information

☆ You may look soft, but you have a strong and determined backbone.

☆ You may be very artistic and musical with a good singing voice, and many Libra rising subjects work as musicians.

☆ You have a really lovely outer manner, and often a lovely inner nature as well.

Libra Rising Celebrities

John McCain
Mohandas K Gandhi
Monica Lewinski
Diana Dors
Jose Maria Carreras
Denzel Washington

11

Scorpio

Ruled by Pluto

Give me more Love, or more Disdain;
the Torrid, or the Frozen Zone
Bring equal ease unto my paine:
The Temperate affords me none:
Either extreme, of Love or Hate,
Is sweeter than a calme estate.
Thomas Carew Mediocrity in Love Rejected

This is a fixed sign, which implies the ability to stay with a situation and see it through, and it's a water sign, which suggests deep emotions. This is also a sign of long ascension, so there should be plenty of you around.

Early Experiences
Many Scorpio rising children are shy, cautious and rather withdrawn, so they hide their emotions behind a poker face or a blank stare. This makes them hard to read and hard to get close to, which in turn may cut them off from others. If you felt ignored when you were young, think back to the way you behaved towards others. Did you attempt to reach out to people? Did you take any interest in their needs or did you simply hide behind your mask, living inside your own head, interested only in your own dreams and desires?

This is not an easy rising sign, and there will always be residual resentment and even hatred towards those who hurt you when you were younger. There may also be a fear of abandonment, or even loss through people dying around you. Many scenarios can cause this underlying anxiety, but here are a few that people have told me about. Some subjects were born during a war or within a couple of years of a death in the family. Some were afraid of one or both parents or others who looked after them. Some were abused, talked down to, battered or sexually mistreated. Many had at least one drunken parent, or one who had a weak character or poor health. Whatever the circumstances, you learned early to keep your feelings under control and never allow your face to betray the thoughts inside. This retreat behind the mask, the closed-face withdrawal, is the classic benchmark of this rising sign. One subject told me that when she was nine years old, her drunken bully of a father died, and she had to pretend to be sad and upset, and then she continued to keep her feelings about her father away from other family members. In some cases, a nice parent dies and another adult comes along and causes problems.

You may have different values and priorities from the rest of your family, and these differing values could have consisted of almost anything. Perhaps your parents wanted a humdrum existence, while you yearned for something more exciting and more meaningful. I've come across Scorpio rising subjects who left their parental home at the first opportunity because it was boring and stultifying, mentally and physically cramped, or financially or academically impoverished. Girls with this rising sign often escape into an early relationship and motherhood.

There are individuals who got on famously with their families while they were small, only to experience difficulties as they began to grow up, at which point they leave home or are thrown out. Some are happy at home but experience problems at school, while others loved school and used it as an escape from home life. One girl's family moved from country to country, so she was always a stranger in school, and unable to speak the language or understand what was going on. This business of moving from one country to another and having to start again in an environment where you don't know the rules is not unusual for this sign.

The key to this sign is resentment about something that didn't work properly. One girl had a large dog that went with her everywhere, and she and the dog stayed out of the home as much as possible. This was because a bedridden, senile old grandfather lived in the only living room. Another had a useless agoraphobic mother and a father who never spoke to her. Another was the only person in the household who spoke English, so she was expected to deal with her feckless father's legal problems.

Some have a brother or sister who is favoured while they themselves can do nothing right. Understandably, many people with this rising sign prefer animals to human beings.

This rising sign is frequently involved with handicaps of one kind or another. I've come across too many instances for it to be more coincidence. There are Scorpio rising subjects who are mentally or physically handicapped from birth, and others who start out normal, but by dint of accident, disease or even by their choice of lifestyle, become restricted in some way later. Others bring up handicapped children themselves. Your weird childhood leads to you developing a powerful level of intuition, which serves you well throughout life.

Appearance
Remember to make allowances for racial differences, family tendencies and the influence of the rest of your birthchart when looking at astrological appearances.

You have good features and great hair and you look wonderful in photographs. You have a lovely smile that lights up your whole face, but you have to know someone a little before you favour them with one of your lovely grins. You are light on your feet and a naturally good dancer, but as you get older, you have to guard against too much sitting about, as you can gain weight. Your best feature is your voice, as it's low and oddly captivating. It commands respect and it sounds sexy. You may have a hawk-like face with a penetrating gaze, or a flat, slightly oriental look and a vaguely puzzled expression that gives little away.

Outer Manner
You have some special ability or interest which makes you stand out from other people. This slight studiousness, coupled with your diffidence, makes you appear clever and mysterious. You don't push yourself forward in social situations, and you are at your most relaxed when working on your own particular hobbies.

It's always a joy to sit quietly and listen to you when you relax and open out and you have a wonderful sense of humour. Your company is so good that time spent with you goes by quickly. You are curious about the motives and behaviour of other people and you may tend to put total strangers under interrogation; some Scorpio rising subjects can appear abrupt and forbidding, critical, offensive and rather frightening.

The Midheaven
The midheaven shows the subject's aims and ambitions, his public standing and his attitude to work outside the home. It can often throw

light on strange or unexpected behaviour in a way that even the Sun, Moon and Ascendant don't always address. Some rising signs usually have only one possible MC, while others can have two or even three possible MCs, depending on the time of year in which a person was born, along with the hemisphere and latitude of birth.

In the UK and similar northerly latitudes, the MC is almost equally split between Leo and Virgo. In the USA and southern Europe about two thirds of the MC will be in Leo, with the remainder in Virgo. Either MC will make the subject cautiously ambitious, but the drive to achieve will be directed differently.

Scorpio/Leo
If you lose your job or suffer a setback that calls for a close look at your situation and your potential, you can view it as a tragedy, and you harbour a deep and abiding resentment for the person or organisation that cost you your career. However, your tremendous reserves of courage and energy ensure that you don't wallow in misery for long, but soon get up and make a fresh start.

The fixed nature of this sign makes you reliable and efficient, and the Scorpio motto is, 'if you are going to do a job, do it properly'. You are thorough and painstaking and you hate to be rushed and hassled. The Leo MC gives you a desire for status and glamour, while the Scorpio ascendant adds caution, tenacity and independence, therefore you head slowly towards the top, stamping your personal style upon your surroundings as you go. This combination can also denote a winning athlete or a top psychiatrist. Many of you opt for a career in connection with music. You could go into teaching, banking, coal or diamond mining.

Many of you spend some of your spare time scouting, guiding or something similar, while others are drawn to a military career, which offers you a pseudo family or clan atmosphere. The services provide opportunities for travel and sport, plus the opportunity to develop your natural interest in the vehicles and weapons of war. One Scorpio rising subject of my acquaintance left her awful childhood behind by taking a job on a cruise liner.

Some of you find your way into the police force, because you work well within a team and can command the respect of your comrades. Your investigative powers and natural mistrust of fellow humans stands you in good stead here, while your physical strength and well-trained body enable you to enjoy exercise and combat. Similarly, you may go into medicine or become a paramedic. These careers are useful to the community at large, offering aid and protection to the weak, and thus allowing you to express the powerful 'knight in shining armour' aspect of your personality.

Scorpio/Virgo

This combination should lead you towards a medical career, or at least towards a strong interest in all aspects of mental and physical healing. The Scorpio/Virgo combination includes surgeons, doctors, herbalists, spiritual healers and psychiatrists. There is a desire to help humanity and at the same time a fascination with human and animal biology and perhaps even with mental and physical pain. You may prefer a career in the background, as a civil servant, secretary or social worker. You could choose to work in the food or the clothing industry or even in the meat trade. These jobs supply basic needs to the public. Other choices can include acting, spiritual healing, alternative therapies and hypnotherapy. You need a career that matters and that allows you to feel as if you count for something. It's also worth remembering that Scorpio is associated with sex, therefore, rape crisis counselling may appeal to you, as might gynaecology.

The midheaven can sometimes indicate the type of person to whom you are attracted both as working partners and as lovers, so you might find yourself most comfortable alongside Leo and Virgo people.

The Descendant

In this case, the seventh house cusp is in Taurus. When you find the right partner, you settle down to a long-lived and very affectionate relationship, but even this relationship is not without fireworks. It's also worth noting that your most successful relationship is likely to be a second or subsequent marriage, after you have learned a bit about living with others. You may experiment with a sexy firebrand on one occasion and a gentle, uncritical homemaker the next.

You enjoy becoming a parent, although you may have some unrealistic ideas of what it means to bring up children. It's worth remembering that the fifth house is concerned with children, and yours is in the illusory and delusory sign of Pisces.

If your partner were the Taurean type, you share a love of music and the sensual joys of good food and good sex, but you both have powerful and destructive tempers. If you are not too uncompromising in outlook and the rest of your chart includes some lighter factors, they can work out very well. You take commitments seriously, and that's an advantage.

Love and Relating

Scorpio on the chart has a reputation for sexiness, but while some Scorpio risers are sexy, others aren't particularly interested. You may be very keen on sex at some times of your life and uninterested at others. You may choose to remain celibate for religious reasons, or because you wish to save your strength for the athletic field or the boxing ring. Some of you will do anything where sex is concerned, while others are fastidious and inhibited.

Some of you really get off on fights and nasty atmospheres, and the casual violence of your marriages can destroy your children. If you feel threatened or maltreated, you enter into a war of attrition for years until one of you suddenly decides enough is enough and walks out. You take offence even at the most helpful, well-meant and constructive criticism, but you can be an expert at dishing it out. You soon learn just which of your partner's buttons to push. Scorpio risers need a partner who stands up to them or who lets their drama and attitude go in one ear and out the other. Having said all the above, many of you are the most loving, caring and sensitive of partners. There's just no middle road where you are concerned.

Many male Scorpio risers marry large, motherly women. You need affection, reassurance and a feeling of continuity. You appreciate acceptance, even by your spouse's family and you benefit greatly from a wise partner who encourages you to open out and express yourself. If you have the kind of partner who includes you in the mainstream of their life, who genuinely respects your opinions and wants your company, you are the best, the most loyal and hardworking mate in the whole zodiac.

There may be something odd where children are concerned, because you may have children that you don't want or you may not be able to have ones that you do want. You may leave parenthood until late in life, or take on someone else's children.

Health

The uterus and related areas can present problems, while the male organs may suffer hernias and prostate gland difficulties. Vasectomies can go wrong and there may be something wrong with the sperm count. Scorpio risers can become ill very quickly and very dramatically from time to time. When this happens you instantly become an excellent patient (at least as far as the doctors and hospital are concerned). You respond well to treatment and soon forget that you were ever very ill. Heart trouble is surprisingly common, as are stomach ulcers as result of unreleased stress and tension. Many of you suffer from time to time with problems related to the ears, sinuses, teeth and throat. Many of you also suffer from back problems.

Additional Information

☆ You think and feel deeply, and you are a good person with whom to talk things over.

☆ Many of you love animals, so you might make a career in that area.

☆ You may also be into conservation and alternative forms of energy or alternative lifestyles.

☆ You may have brushed up against death and loss while you were very young.

☆ You have a sexy outer image, but this may not reflect the real you.

☆ You aren't good in an emergency; unless you are specifically trained to deal with sudden, unexpected problems, you can get into a flap and lose your temper.

Scorpio Rising Celebrities

Clint Eastwood
Patrick Macnee
Claudia Schiffer
Margaret Thatcher
Edith Piaf
Johnny Carson

12

Sagittarius

Ruled by Jupiter

Slav, Teuton, Kelt, I count them all
My friends and brother souls,
With all the peoples, great and small,
That wheel between the poles
You, Canadian, Indian,
Australasian, African,
All your hearts be in harmony!
Alfred Lord Tennyson

Sagittarius is a mutable sign, which implies the ability to adapt to changing circumstances. It's also a fire sign, which suggests that you catch on quickly and you do things quickly. This is a sign of medium-to-long ascension, which means that there are plenty of you around.

Early Experiences
You appear to have been born easily and to have been a wanted child, but your childhood was patchy, with parts of it being good and some parts being diabolical. You learned early in life to switch off and avoid things you dislike. Your parents may have separated from each other. There could have been problems that were beyond your control, such as a deteriorating relationship between your parents. There may have been conflict between you and your parents. The chances are that even now, you love your family but prefer to live at a distance from them.

You could have found your father too fussy, disciplinarian or prejudiced for your freewheeling taste. There may have been regular rows about the state of your room, your performance at school or your lack of application to some special interest that consumed your parents ('We spent all that money on violin lessons and now look at you, all you want to do is go fishing...!'). Your parents may have objected to your tendency to disappear whenever some boring chore loomed up on the horizon, or they may have felt relieved when you did disappear, because it offered them a welcome respite from arguments. Your relationship with your father is ambivalent, because you may have hated him while you were young, but developed respect for him later on. You may have loved and understood him, but never learned to communicate with him except by getting into yet another shouting match.

Your relationship with your mother is even worse. You may have seen her as the servant of the family who lived her life in a particularly old-fashioned and limited manner. You may have considered her stupid, useless or powerless. The view of your mother as a person who was incapable of making a decision would inevitably reinforce your natural desire for self-determination and independence. Later in life, you may have come to understand the difficulties under which she lived and the compromises that she had to make, but even now, you may lack any real respect for her. Whatever the circumstances, you felt cramped, restricted and even immobilised. It's possible that you were disadvantageously compared to a brother or sister and maybe you felt that you were growing up in a town or an area that was small, dull and far from the action. Maybe you were expected to follow a strict religious regime in which you had no personal belief, or to conform to a restrictive set of values. Maybe your home life was great, but financial or cultural impoverishment irritated you.

Somewhere along the line, you switched off, tuned out and began to look outside the home for some kind of escape route. Many of you realised that education could offer you a useful way out, so you were quick to latch on at school, which earned you the praise of your teachers and the admiration of your peers. You were unlikely to be the victim of bullying, due to your strong wiry frame and your natural aggression. For some of you therefore, school gave you the precious gift of early success and the opportunity to develop a sense of self-esteem. As you passed the point of puberty, your eyes and thoughts were drawn ever more outward to the wider world, and sooner or later, you left home – and may even have left the country.

Appearance

Remember to make allowances for racial differences, family tendencies and the influence of the rest of your birthchart when looking at astrological appearances.

If you are typical, you are medium height, slim and raw-boned, with the characteristically long jaw and brilliant smile. Some chubby and round-faced Sagittarius rising subjects have unusually attractive hair and eyes. Sagittarius rising women are often top-heavy, with rounded shoulders and a large bust. White races often have golden or reddish hair.

Outer Manner

You are friendly, cheerful and outgoing, and you lack caution and fear when meeting new people. Some of you are in a permanent whirl, chasing around like a demented white rabbit, while others affect a superior, know-it-all attitude. Some of you have a slow-moving, leisurely manner that belies the quickness of your mind. You are curious about people and therefore may subject perfect strangers to the third degree. This is usually done quite innocently, because you do not intend to hurt anybody. Every new person or situation offers you delightful opportunities to further your knowledge. You try to fit in with any company in which you find yourself, whilst actually remaining a distinct individual. You may appear eccentric to strangers, especially conventional ones, but the messages you transmit on first acquaintance are usually cheerful and friendly. You may have a knack for making tactless remarks, but you are also very funny and you love to make people laugh.

The Midheaven

The midheaven shows the subject's aims and ambitions, his public standing and his attitude to work outside the home. It can often throw light on strange or unexpected behaviour in a way that even the Sun, Moon and Ascendant don't always address. Some rising signs usually have only one possible MC, while others can have two or even three possible MCs, depending on the time of year in which a person was born, along with the hemisphere and latitude of birth.

In the UK, and similar northerly latitudes, those of you whose ascendant is in a very early degree of Sagittarius will have a Virgo midheaven, while those of you whose ascendant is in the very last degrees of the sign will have a Scorpio MC. In fact, the majority of you have a Libran MC. In the USA and southern Europe, about one third of you have Virgo on the mid-heaven, while the remainder have Libra on the MC.

Many of us are attracted to people whose Sun sign is the same as our MC.

Sagittarius/Virgo

This combination produces an adaptable person who is also very idealistic. You have a strong need to serve mankind, either on an individual basis by caring for an elderly or handicapped relative, or on a group basis by working in one of the caring professions. Some of you work for a charity or for some other idealistic movement. Subjects with this MC may choose to work as teachers, social workers and probation officers or in some aspect of the medical profession. The travel and transport industries are popular (remember, Virgo is ruled by restless Mercury), but you may also be drawn to farming, veterinary work or anything connected with animal welfare. You could help people to keep on looking good by working in the cosmetics or clothing industries. You may be into vegetarianism or good nutrition. This combination makes for a very nervy and restless personality, but the attention to details that is Virgo coupled with the Sagittarian imagination and optimism can create outstanding success in any profession.

Sagittarius/Libra

By far the bulk of Sagittarius rising subjects come into this category. You are drawn to ambitious projects and large-scale ideas that can be extremely successful. Both Sagittarius and Libra are concerned with advocacy and both signs like to see justice done, so a legal career is a possibility. You could be equally drawn to spiritual ideas that lead you into a religious or philosophical way of life. Even if you don't become directly involved in the spiritual world, an element of this will enter your everyday life. The worlds of astrology or psychic matters might appeal to you. Sagittarius rising subjects are highly intuitive and often very psychic. The desire to help humanity in a more practical way could lead you into politics.

Many teachers have this combination on their charts, as it's naturally Libran to give advice, and another traditionally Sagittarian interest is long distance travel; there are many of you working as couriers, travel agents, translators and airline pilots. You get on well with most people and have no prejudice towards foreigners. In fact, you enjoy meeting people from different cultures and looking into different ways of life. Last but not least, many of you find your way into show business. You are a natural actor and comedian, and probably a good singer or dancer too, so you could spend your life actually working in the business, or you could spend a few years on the stage before settling down to a normal career. Many of you retain your interest in stage work and may even return to it later in life.

Here are a few real life Sagittarius rising examples (with names changed). Jennie is a highly qualified computer expert who also lectures at the University of Sussex. Every Sunday or religious holiday you will find her singing in her local Church choir. Robert is a teacher who spent a couple of years acting before taking his degree and embarked on his teaching career. John is an electronics buyer who has a degree in drama. Tony is a bank manager who is deeply involved in amateur dramatics. He tells me that when he retires, he will become a full time actor. Mike is a teacher and administrator in adult education, and he is very dramatic and very Welsh. It would be amazing if he hadn't done his share of singing or acting, and Mike has admitted to me that he would have liked to be an actor. You may be good at, and very interested in competitive sports, particularly golf, tennis, yachting and motor racing. Another interest could be the care of animals, especially horses. You may like the horseracing scene.

Sagittarius/Scorpio

Very few people have this combination. Such a combination stresses the idealistic side of Scorpio, which expresses itself in a need to heal. You may work in the medical, psychiatric or veterinary fields and you may be a gifted spiritual healer. Your powerful intuition and psychic ability lead you to take an interest in spiritual and psychic matters. The legal interests that are common in Sagittarians might be used directly in forensic work of some kind. You have more patience and determination than the other two types, which suggests that you could haul yourself slowly up to a position of great authority and responsibility. You would use your powerful gifts both wisely and firmly.

You are an excellent communicator, so you could find work in journalism, radio or television. You like advising and helping the public, so a media career could well be a very good idea for you. A sporting career is also possible, as many of you are excellent sportsmen and women who can make the grade professionally.

The Descendant

The opposite point to the ascendant is the descendant, which traditionally shows the type of person to whom we are attracted. In the case of a Sagittarian ascendant, the descendant is in Gemini. These two signs have even more in common with each other than most ascendant / descendant combinations, so you either get on well with Geminis, or find them extremely irritating. Being idealistic and highly-strung, you need a placid and practical partner to create a balanced relationship. Geminis can be practical when making or fixing things, but they are far too nervous, critical, restrictive and whiny for you to cope with. You desperately need the support of a stable home and family environment, but you may have the awkward habit of keeping two relationships on the go at once, which could make life just a little bit too crowded for comfort.

You need freedom in any relationship, and are also prepared to allow your partner to have the opportunity to be a person in his or her own right. You can be cold hearted at times, even to the point of cutting off completely from other people and disappearing inside yourself. As long as you have a measure of friendship in any relationship, you can usually make a success of it.

Love and Relating

You are a relater and you need company, so you marry young, but you may be too unsettled and unstable to stay married for long the first time round. Later on, you can form a surprisingly stable marriage, due to your ability to choose a fairly self-reliant partner, although I suspect that male Sagittarius rising subjects are luckier in this respect than female ones.

Sexually, you like to experiment, and curiosity could be the main reason for your numerous sexual partners. Later in life, when some of your curiosity has been satisfied, you settle down more easily to family life. You are one of those people who can actually live quite happily without sex, as long as your creative urges are being satisfied, although you do need attention and affection. You were not cuddled enough as a child and you really do enjoy the sensation of being held and cared for by another. You can also offset any missing sex by pouring out your energies into sports, hobbies and even the Church. To be honest, sex isn't your biggest problem: your worst enemy is boredom.

As far as friendship is concerned, you can be here today and gone tomorrow. Your friendly, open nature ensures that you make friends easily enough, but you tend to drift away and forget them when you move on to other things.

Health

You are either extremely healthy or extremely unfit. To be honest, the chances are that you are rarely ill, but if you do go through a bad patch, it can last for quite a few years before you return to full health. You suffer from sporting injuries and silly accidents due to the speed at which you move. Your vulnerable spots are your hips, pelvic area and your thighs, so arthritis, accidents to the legs, and problems related to the femoral artery are possible, while women may suffer from womb troubles. Your nerves can let you down, giving you sleepless nights, skin and stomach problems, if your ascendant is late in Sagittarius, you could have allergies to certain kinds of food and drink.

Additional Information

☆ You may spend time in care, in boarding school or for some other reason, away from the family when young.

☆ You may have a reasonable home life but a poor experience of school life. However, you enjoy learning and you are bound to take courses or learn things for fun later in life.

☆ Your mother may have been critical, demanding, a whiner, cold hearted, money minded or a complete pain in the neck. Either or both parents could have been drunks, druggies or in some other way, useless. Alternatively, they could have been perfectly fine but boring.

☆ You are extremely capable and talented. You could practically build a house with your own hands, learn anything and do anything. Indeed, you are better at solving practical problems than emotional ones.

☆ One unforgivable fault that I've discovered in those with Sagittarius either as a Sun sign or a rising sign is the way you lash out in a particularly hurtful and thoughtless manner if you feel inadequate, and sadly, you can do this when nobody has any intention of criticising or harming you.

☆ Truly, your cheerful outer nature and great sense of humour draw people to you very easily, but one can't help wondering how long they stay enamoured of you, once they experience your sharp tongue.

<u>Sagittarius Rising Celebrities</u>

John Galsworthy
Sylvester Stallone
Bob Dylan
Elvis Presley
Elizabeth Taylor
Marlon Brando

13

Capricorn

Ruled by Saturn

Nothing to do but work,
Nothing to eat but food,
Nothing to wear but clothes
To keep one from going nude.
Benjamin Franklin King, The Pessimist

This is an earth sign that's also cardinal in nature, which implies the desire to make things happen, along with the patience and determination to make sure that they do. Capricorn is also feminine/negative in nature, implying introversion and shyness. This is a sign of short ascension, which means that, as far as births in northern latitudes are concerned, there are not many of you about.

Early Experiences

Capricorn rising denotes a difficult birth or a difficult situation surrounding your entry into the world. One could theorise that, because Capricorn is associated with old age, you will have been through a number of previous incarnations, and knowing what is ahead, you don't really want to go through it all over again! Whatever the theory, your mother's labour may have been protracted, painful and dangerous, or difficult in some other way. One such subject told me that she had been born fairly easily, but the birth took place in an ambulance halfway across Ealing Common, in the middle of one of the worst bombing raids of World War Two!

Many Capricorn rising subjects are born to older parents who didn't expect to have a child at that stage of their lives. A woman called Paula told me that her mother was 43 years old when she had a very bad attack of indigestion after eating pickled onions. The attack was so severe that her mother paid a visit to her doctor the next day. He told her that she was in the late stages of pregnancy, and two weeks later, Paula was born. The birth itself wasn't too difficult, but it was worrying, partly due to her mother's age, and also because there was so little time to get anything organised, and shortly after this event, her father had his first really serious nervous breakdown. The sign of Capricorn is traditionally assumed to be a sad one, indicative of a life filled with limitations and hard lessons. There is some truth in this idea, particularly during childhood and youth, but the problems are more likely to stem from difficult circumstances than from cruel or unloving parents. This emphasis on hard circumstances is the benchmark of this rising sign.

One of your parents, probably your father, may have been a distant figure, either because he was naturally reserved or withdrawn, or because his work took up a lot of his time. Your mother might have been strict but not unreasonable or uncaring towards you. Circumstances dictated that you remain quietly in the background, making very few demands and behaving in an adult manner while you were still very young. I always think of this as an old-fashioned sign, because it's associated with the kind of childhoods that were far more common in years gone by. This ascendant is probably found more often in third world societies where opportunities for happiness or for creativity in childhood are still unobtainable luxuries. During your childhood, your parents may have been short of time and money. There may have been too many mouths for them to feed, financial setbacks or family illness. You may have had a parent or a sibling who had some physical or mental handicap. You could have had an early introduction to the sadder side of life by losing a family member in a particularly tragic manner, and it's very likely that you spent a lot of time with grandparents or other older people.

It's possible that your parents themselves had risen from obscurity to wealth, and if one or even both of your parents were especially successful, courageous or outstanding, you may have found this too hard an act to follow. The effects of this childhood could have led to a number of different reactions on your part, depending upon your basic nature. One possibility is that you followed in their footsteps; another is that you gave up the unequal battle and dropped out. A third possibility is that you followed a completely different path, finding sound values that are very different from those of your parents.

You were shy and withdrawn and inclined to hang back and let others step forward and take all the glory. You had little confidence in yourself and you may have been afraid of one or more of the adults around you, either because there was a genuine threat to your safety, or because of vague fears and phobias. You were finely built and small for your age, and thus unable to compete with larger, tougher children, either on the sports field or in any kind of physical violence. You were a delicate and timid child, and your health may have been poor. You were not easy to bring up. The fact that you survived at all says a lot about your inner resources of courage and determination. You didn't give up on life, and you learned the value of self-control. Despite this inauspicious start, you are friendly, sociable and cheerful. You are not flamboyant, but you are chatty and even a bit flirty when it's appropriate to be so.

Appearance

Remember to make allowances for racial differences, family tendencies and the influence of the rest of your birthchart when looking at astrological appearances.

The chances are that if you have Capricorn rising, you will have rather bony features, with high cheekbones, large eyes and a nice, if slightly toothy smile. You may smile with the corners of your mouth turned downwards rather than upwards, whilst at the same time lighting up your eyes. Your hair is your worst feature, because it's sparse, fine and nondescript. Men with this rising sign become thin on top. Women spend a fortune in the hairdresser, while cursing this ever-present bane of their lives. Your height and physique are small to medium. You could put on a little weight as you get older, but generally speaking, you will remain perhaps just a little below average in height and weight. You choose conservative clothes - either city-smart outfits or cheap and cheerful, according to your lifestyle and your pocket. To be honest, you don't give much attention to your clothing unless there is a special occasion.

Outer Manner

You are the last person to push yourself to the forefront in any kind of new situation. You appear calm, quiet, gentle and modest in social situations, whilst in business situations you are formal and businesslike. The signals you send out to new acquaintances are gentle, kind and practical. You rarely express your feelings publicly, and you are a past master at the art of being non-committal. You go out of your way to make others feel comfortable, but you are reserved. Your dry sense of humour is always a delightful discovery to any new acquaintance, and your genuinely non-hostile approach to the world ensures that you are surprisingly popular. You are a good conversationalist; partly because you usually have something interesting to talk about, but mainly because you are a good and caring listener.

The Midheaven

The midheaven shows the subject's aims and ambitions, his public standing and his attitude to work outside the home. It can often throw light on strange or unexpected behaviour in a way that even the Sun, Moon and Ascendant don't always address. Some rising signs usually have only one possible MC, while others can have two or even three possible MCs, depending on the time of year in which a person was born, along with the hemisphere and latitude of birth.

In northern latitudes such as the UK, the majority of you will have your midheaven in Scorpio, while those of you whose ascendant is in the last couple of degrees of Capricorn will have Sagittarius on the midheaven. In the case of births in the USA and southern areas of Europe, those who have the first few degrees of Capricorn rising will have the midheaven in Libra, whilst the rest will have the MC in Scorpio.

The sign on the MC can sometimes denote the type of person whom you enjoy either working or living alongside.

Capricorn/Libra

Both of these signs are cardinal in nature, which suggests that you prefer to make your own decisions, although you are fairly co-operative in working partnerships. The Libran MC modifies your Capricorn rising shyness. You could become a capable travel agent, personnel officer or financial adviser. You have a natural affinity for figures, which is useful, whatever your line of work. The Libran midheaven gives you an artistic outlook, good looks and good dress sense, so you shine in situations that require good presentation. You may not excel as a creative innovator, but you are excellent at judging the work of others. You can see at a glance what will work and what will not, and it's this critical faculty that could successfully take you into the world of fashion or publishing. You have some sales ability, but not the pushy kind.

Capricorn/Scorpio

It's possible that you would be drawn to the Scorpio interests of medicine or police work, where your careful, methodical mind would come in handy, but if you decide to eschew these careers in favour of an ordinary job, you would do it with energy and diligence. You can be relied upon to do a job thoroughly, so long as nobody rushes or pressurises you. Your best bet is to tackle one job at a time and do it properly. The Scorpio MC could take you into some kind of research work, and you could also make a good investigative journalist or scientific author. You may become interested in coins, stamps and antique silver, where your memory for details and hallmarks come to your aid. You have to take care that your outer manner doesn't offend others, especially at an interview or when trying to get information out of others. You may put on an aggressive or hostile front in order to hide your vulnerability, but remember that others will take you at face value, and thereby miss your finer qualities. The Scorpio affinity with liquids could take you into the oil industry or shipping. I've known one such subject work worked as a cleaner at a public swimming baths.

Capricorn/Sagittarius

This rare combination really doesn't fit comfortably, because the two signs have little in common, but it could make you a pretty powerful character. You may be drawn into teaching or caring for others, possibly by going into the world of probation, prisons and the law. Your practical idealism might lead you into alternative forms of medicine, counselling or even astrology. Your interest in travel and business could lead you to work for an airline or to set up a postal courier service. Alternatively, you could go into some kind of religious occupation or even become a professional mystic or a kind of businesslike Yogi.

The Descendant

The opposite point to the ascendant is the descendant. This is traditionally supposed to show the type of person to whom we are attracted. In the case of Capricorn rising, the descendant is in Cancer, which goes a long way towards accounting for the Capricorn love of family life. I have no evidence to suggest that you would go out of your way to choose a Cancerian partner, but I guess that if you did, all else being equal, the match would work well; the signs have a great deal in common, both being interested in families and also in business.

However, the emotionalism and moodiness of the Cancerian might irritate you after a while and the combination of these two signs might lead to too much negativity and gloom in the relationship.

On the whole, the Cancerian descendant makes you good towards all those with whom you associate, be they friends, neighbours or working partners, and you hate to let anyone down. One black mark that could spoil some of your relationships is your tendency to be stingy about small matters. You could be the type who complains about your partner's use of hot water or the way he squeezes the toothpaste tube. However, if your partner is financially independent, fairly thick-skinned or also rather tight-fisted, none of this will be a problem.

Love and Relating

This is where contradictions enter the scene. You are able to live without sex when it's not available, and you may do so due to shyness, fastidiousness or a quite reasonable fear of jumping into bed with someone to whom you haven't been properly introduced! When you are with someone you love, you can really let your hair down. Remember, this is an earth sign, so it implies sensuousness. You may be flirtatious, but your strong sense of propriety, not to mention self-preservation, will probably prevent too much actual tomfoolery.

Health

You may suffer from rheumatism, especially in your knees. Other typical problems are tinnitus or deafness, possibly associated with some kind of bone problem in the ears. Your difficult childhood may leave you with nervous ailments, such as asthma, eczema and psoriasis, together with chesty ailments such as bronchitis. Despite these annoying problems, Capricorns traditionally live to a ripe old age.

Additional Information

☆ You can be surprisingly talkative when with people you trust. You read a lot and love books, and because of this, you have a lot of knowledge and information inside your head.

☆ You may enjoy working as a sales person or an agent of some kind. You are sensible with money and good in business, but you are not a risk taker.

☆ Some Capricorn rising subjects come from very poor or deprived backgrounds, but then pull themselves upwards by sheer hard work.

☆ Sometimes the poverty and lack of intellectual stimulus are due to parents who are immigrants from some less developed culture, or being born into a situation where there were few opportunities to get on in life.

Capricorn Rising Celebrities

Liberace
Jane Fonda
Sean Connery
Lucille Ball
John Belushi
Candice Bergan

14

Aquarius

Ruled by Uranus

These things shall be! A loftier race
Than e'er the world hath known, shall rise,
With flame of knowledge in their souls
And light of knowledge in their eyes.
    John Addington Symonds (English Critic), New and Old. A Vista

This is an air sign that's also fixed in nature, so you are clever and tenacious. If you become attached to an idea, or accustomed to a particular way of life, you will not willingly change your mind. Aquarius is masculine and positive in nature, which denotes extroversion and courage. This is a sign of short ascension, which means that in northern latitudes, there are not many of you around.

Early Experiences

Aquarius is the least predictable sign of the zodiac, so it's almost impossible to generalise about any aspect of your life. There may have been some kind of dramatic or unexpected event that disrupted your life, possibly due to war or some other outside circumstance, but this may have turned out for the best in some way. One Aquarius rising subject told me that, as a result of wartime evacuation, he received a far better education and indeed, a far better childhood than he would otherwise have had. This element of unpredictability is the hallmark of this rising sign.

You were a clever child, but you may not have made much effort at school, yet you catch up later in life and you do very well in your chosen sphere of work. Despite your inability to be cajoled or coerced, you longed for parental approval, especially from your father. You may have had an excellent relationship with one parent and a prickly, uncomfortable one with the other. Either parent might have been moody, resentful, childish and unpredictable. In a normal childhood, you could have been subject to periods of unexplained withdrawal of parental affection. If your home situation was pleasant, you would have been aware of events within the family circle that appeared to be beyond anyone's control. Your school life could have been disrupted, probably due to your family moving around a good deal. Some subjects don't do well at school, but take up an interest later at which they excel. Some find it hard to concentrate on anything for long, or grasp new concepts quickly, and then lose interest again just as quickly.

Here are a couple of examples of Aquarius rising children learning how fragile life can be. Edwin's parents had a second child when he was eight years old, and this younger brother was born with a severe mental handicap. In another example, Jack was terribly upset when his father became ill with a heart condition, but fortunately, a coronary by-pass gave his father a further 22 years of life. It's interesting to note that the sign of Aquarius is associated with new and experimental ideas, and at that time, by-pass surgery was so new that it was experimental!

Even as a small child, you needed freedom, space, and you also needed to be on the move, so you were rarely indoors for long. You had friends all over the place, and couldn't wait to shoot off out of the house to see them. Yet, you needed to know that everything was all right at home and in your own private world before you could go exploring.

There may have been very little pattern to your life. Your parents might have changed their attitude to you from one day to another or they may have handed out confusing psychological messages. For example they may have told you that they believed in total honesty, whilst fiddling the taxman and pinching stuff from their place of work. If your parents were reasonable, they may have been thoroughly unconventional. Perhaps one of your parents was particularly successful or gifted. Maybe one of them was a total failure or even a drunken wreck. You yourself were a jumpy, nervy child, being prone to nervous ailments and bouts of peculiar behaviour. If your parents were all right, they would have found you difficult to bring up, and if they were not, it's a miracle that you survived at all!

Appearance

Remember to make allowances for racial differences, family tendencies and the influence of the rest of your birthchart when looking at astrological appearances.

You are good looking. Aquarian women learn to use cosmetics well, because their complexion is pale or sallow. The bone structure of your face is strong, and you have a big smile, so you photograph well. Your eyes are probably quite ordinary, plain brown and slightly prominent, but not especially large. However, your highly arched eyebrows draw attention to your eyes, making them look larger than they actually are. Your nose is prominent (maybe bent or twisted) and your teeth regular and very white, so your smile is great.

The effect of these well-developed features, with your humourous expression, gives you a strong and effective appearance. Your hair may be your worst feature, being a dull brown or turning grey when you are still very young. You may be only of average height, or on the tall side.

Your choice of clothes is totally individual and possibly even totally outrageous! You may be the very picture of the smartly dressed businessperson or a complete slob. You may restrict yourself to one colour, for example, never wearing anything but mauve, or you may choose to wear clothes of a bygone age. Most of you prefer casual clothes such as jeans and sweaters. You hate frills, patterns and bunches of flowers on your clothing, and you are far happier wearing strong plain colours. However, you could easily turn up at a formal function in a frockcoat and Red Indian headdress!

Outer Manner

Your manner is friendly, open and non-hostile, unless you are faced with someone who is offensive or unpleasant, in which case, you give him or her absolutely no quarter. You speak your mind and don't fear the consequences. You may be a little shy when you are in an unfamiliar social setting, but once you feel at home, you join in with whatever is going on.

You are a real asset to a village fete! You love meeting new people, and are not at all put off by unusual ones. Your judgement of people is excellent, and you seem to be able to see through surface impressions to the reality that lies underneath. You don't judge people by outer appearances and you cannot be taken in by anyone who puts on airs and graces. Your own approach, apart from being friendly, is businesslike and humourous, but not pushy. In some circumstances, you can appear arrogant, or you may give the impression that you class yourself above the people with whom you associate. When you are with people with whom you are really comfortable, especially if the occasion is a social one, you are terrific. You mix with everyone, thoroughly enjoy yourself and help others to do the same. Your most outstanding qualities are your quick wit and sense of humour. Aquarius risers are the masters of the pithy comment and the hilarious one liner.

The Midheaven

The midheaven shows the subject's aims and ambitions, his public standing and his attitude to work outside the home. It can often throw light on strange or unexpected behaviour in a way that even the Sun, Moon and Ascendant don't always address. Some rising signs usually have only one possible MC, while others can have two or even three possible MCs depending upon the time of year in which a person was born, along with the hemisphere and latitude of birth.

In Britain and other northern hemisphere areas, you will have Sagittarius on the MC, but in other parts of the world, you could have Libra or Scorpio on the MC.

Aquarius/Libra

You are broadminded and very sociable. Your wonderful people skills could take you into politics, business, sales or the law, and you could become a spokesperson for a pressure group. You may go into broadcasting or the press. You like the good life, a good home, nice food, great clothes and possessions, and you learn that the only way to have these things is to overcome your natural tendency to laziness and to go for the kind of job that will bring you a good income. You are very loving and your intentions are good, but you may be too flirtatious and unsettled for marriage or long-term relationships, while your great looks and zest for life bring you many short-term lovers.

Aquarius/Scorpio

You are extremely intelligent and you are a deep thinker who can't accept anything on face value alone, so you will always research those things that interest you. Your working life will include some level of idealism, so you may work in an engineering or business environment, but some aspect of the work ultimately helps humanity, cares for animals, or preserves the planet. You may be attracted to the world of medicine or alternative health, but your high level of intuition and probable psychic ability could take you into the world of spiritual healing or mediumship. Other areas are mining, working on oilrigs and other jobs that take you into harsh environments.

Aquarius/Sagittarius

You need freedom, and you cannot stand being restricted, dictated to or bullied. You seek out the kind of job that allows you to get out and about and meet a variety of people. Your work will involve you meeting and dealing with people from many countries and cultures, and you enjoy this diversity. You look at the world with fresh eyes and bring exciting new ideas to everything you touch, so you are very useful in solving technical problems. Your obsessive nature can be useful, because when the urge hits, you can toss aside your languor and beaver away at a problem until it is solved.

Although you can succeed in any technical field, the most obvious ones include electronics, telecommunications and computers. You are intelligent and quick on the uptake and you have a good memory, therefore you need a job that stretches your mind. Your interest in scientific research could take you into the fields of physics, medicine or even horticulture, but your balanced mind and natural arbitration skills could lead you into law. You are a skilled negotiator, which could suggest either straightforward legal work or something similar, such as Trades Union negotiations. You may be interested in becoming an agent for writers or performers, where you meet talented and interesting people. You could become an inventor or an imaginative writer, especially if the rest of your birthchart leans that way.

You look laid-back and easy-going, but this is a pose, because you are actually very ambitious and you enjoy status, so you need a good position within your job and a career that makes you an object of admiration and envy. You earn money easily but you spend it just as easily, so you enjoy it rather than pile it up for the future. There will be some attachment to religion or mysticism somewhere in your family, or you may become interested in these things yourself, although you will resist being told what to believe in.

The Descendant

The descendant, or cusp of the seventh house, is traditionally supposed to throw light on our attitudes to partnerships and may even indicate the type of person whom we choose to marry.

In the case of Aquarius rising, the descendant is in Leo. There is no evidence that you are especially attracted to Leos, but you do find them easy to understand, because you have a good deal in common with them. Your personal standards are high; you are proud, dignified, obstinate and tenacious. It's possible that you could work well together, but I doubt whether two such egocentric people could actually manage to live together for very long. In general, you seek a partner who is intelligent, independent and good-looking.

Love and Relating

You find it hard to give reassurance to others, and your detached attitude and tendency to give logical answers to emotional questions can leave your partner feeling misunderstood. You need to guard against too much tenacity in relationships, because you can hang on far too long to the wrong person.

You are very active sexually and you are an inventive and exciting lover. However, the most important ingredients in a relationship for you are intelligence, humour, shared interests and friendship. You may go through an experimental stage where you separate love from sex, having a variety of partners, but once you settle into a permanent relationship, you are the faithful type, as long as your partner treats you decently. You are completely turned off by a lack of personal hygiene. You don't fall in love easily, but when you do, that romantic child-like Leo descendant makes you very loving and romantic.

Health

The traditional weak points for this sign are the ankles, so you must guard against phlebitis, thrombosis and accidents to the feet and ankles. I've discovered that Aquarius rising subjects have a great deal of trouble with their ears, noses and throats, and many suffer from hay fever, asthma and allergies. Some are allergic to Penicillin or other antibiotics. Your teeth are either very good or very bad. You have a nice smile, so it would be wise to cultivate a good dentist. You could also be subject to backache.

Additional Information

☆ You probably travelled a good deal in childhood and during your youth, either because your parents took you on trips with them or because they lived in other countries for a while. This would have been an interesting, beneficial and enjoyable experience for you. You probably still love to travel whenever you can afford to do so.

☆ Your desire to help the underdog could take you into local or national politics, and your ambitious nature could take you to the top of this field. Whatever line of work you choose, you will move upwards and your ambition and ability to work hard will serve you well.

☆ You are often the first person to think up some new idea or concept, so you are a real innovator.

☆ You can present a very unconventional image to the world, which may reflect the real person or just be part of your outer persona.

Aquarius Rising Celebrities

Barack Obama
Larry Hagman
Janis Joplin
Tammy Wynette
Bjorn Borg
Michael J Fox

15

Pisces

Ruled by Neptune

We are the music-makers,
And we are the dreamers of dreams,
Wandering by lone sea-breakers,
And sitting by desolate streams;
Arthur O'Shaughnessy

Pisces is a feminine water sign, which makes you very intuitive. You may be a good sales person or a good businessperson, due to your natural understanding of people and what they want. This sign is mutable, so you will spend your working life dealing with people or with things that come into your life, pass through and move on. In northern latitudes, this is a sign of very short ascension, so there are very few of you around.

Early Experiences
When pregnant with you, your mother may have been unhappy, unhealthy, short of money and in no shape to have a baby, so your entry into the world was difficult and dangerous, and your survival over those first few weeks may have been in doubt. You seem to have entered this world with the remnants of a previous life still clinging to you. Your early life is characterised by loneliness and separation from others, possibly due to sickness. Your father may have been severely incapacitated or he may have been an ineffectual character. He may have died or deserted the family, leaving your mother to cope alone. Your mother was probably strong enough to cope with this, but she may have become tired, embittered or self-pitying.

Some Pisces rising children have very poor health, leading to longish spells in hospital. It's probably only when your ascendant progresses from Pisces into Aries when life starts to take off for you. You may have been so ill at times that you were not expected to recover. You may have spent some time away in hospital or in a special school. Even if you were not sent away, you would have spent a good deal of time alone in bed, reading and thinking, and this enforced withdrawal from life allowed your creativity and your imagination to develop.

Lisa was the fifth child, born prematurely to parents who needed another child like a hole in the head! Incidentally, they went on to have a sixth child who has the Moon in Pisces, and whom they needed even less! Lisa was evacuated during the war and this was not a happy experience for her, as she was lonely and desolate. Soon after returning home, she contracted rheumatic fever, so was sent away once again, this time to a special school for delicate children. It was while Lisa was at this school that she discovered a talent for sport, started to make friends and to enjoy life. Soon after her return to the family, her father left home for good. Lisa told me that she never went short of the basic necessities of life, but there were no luxuries and little love.

Margaret was adopted under peculiar circumstances (money changed hands). Her adoptive parents were neither young enough nor sufficiently competent to handle the reality of bringing up a boisterous child. Margaret spent a good deal of time with a variety of 'aunties' who were cajoled and bribed into looking after her. When she was eight, she had a touch of tuberculosis and was sent away to a school for delicate children. While she was at this school, Margaret discovered a talent for art and sport. The school strongly favoured the outdoor life and introduced Margaret to horticulture, which developed into a life-long passion. Eventually, Margaret came home and she grew even closer to her father; she learned to share his interests in gardening, do-it-yourself and fixing up the car. However, just as this rapport was firmly established, her father had a stroke that left him partially paralysed and unable to speak. Both Lisa and Margaret 'escaped' into marriage while teenagers, and both went on to have a number of children and the inevitable divorce and remarriage later on.

Your health may have been all right, but other difficulties may have arisen. For instance, Michelle told me that her father left, forcing her mother to bring up Michelle and her younger sister on her own. Her mother had to work, of course, but also enjoyed a great social life with many boyfriends, holidays and outings, leaving Michelle in charge both of the household and her younger sister from a very early age. Despite this, Michelle did well at school, learned to speak a number of languages, and she eventually became a courier in the travel trade.

It's just possible that your home life was reasonable, but that you were not on the same wavelength as the rest of the family, so you eventually drifted away and made a life for yourself among like-minded people elsewhere. At school, the only subjects that interested you were sport, art, music and dancing. You may have been bullied at school and thus learned to be suspicious of new people. Later in life, you take courses on the subjects that interested you, and you become quite an authority on those things.

One aspect of your personality that will always set you apart from others is your incredible level of intuition. Indeed, you may be extremely psychic. You will be drawn to such things as crystals and crystal healing, or perhaps psychic art, where you draw pictures of people's spirit guides for them. It's very likely that you read Tarot cards, and perhaps tea leaves.

Another alternative is that you become religious, even to the point of joining some silent order, or getting into some weird cult. Many of you take up Spiritualism or Wicca.

On a more practical note, you are probably very sporty and you might be a very lucky gambler. You could be attracted to the world of health and healing, thus becoming a nurse, doctor or complementary therapist.

Your downfall would be escaping into fantasy or perhaps getting into drugs and alcohol, but if you avoid these pitfalls, you could become a top dancer, actor, sports person, novelist, artist, sculptor or musician.

You could reach the very heights of human existence, or fall to the lowest levels.

Appearance

Remember to make allowances for racial differences, family tendencies and the influence of the rest of your birthchart when looking at astrological appearances.

You should be of medium height and size, with a pale, translucent complexion and fine hair. Your eyes are probably very pale grey or grey-blue in colour and they may be large and lustrous. You are slim when young, but inclined to put on weight later in life. You have a quiet, gentle and humourous voice that's pleasant and relaxing to listen to. Your choice of clothes is casual and sporty, but not especially unusual, and you are not especially self-conscious about your appearance. Oddly enough, you may be fussy about the colour of your clothes, preferring to stick to one or two colours that you like.

Outer Manner

I've come across Pisces rising individuals who are friendly, helpful and pleasant, with a humourous and kindly manner, but too many are unpleasant, hostile, hard and offensive. There may be a kind hearted and loving person under this crusty exterior, but I wonder whether many people are prepared to hang around long enough to find out.

The Midheaven

The midheaven can show the individual's aims and ambitions, his public standing and his attitude to work outside the home. It can often throw light on strange or unexpected behaviour in a way that even the Sun, Moon and Ascendant don't always address. Some rising signs usually have only one possible MC, while others can have two or even three possible MCs, depending upon the time of year in which a person was born, along with the hemisphere and latitude of birth.

In the northern hemisphere, Pisces rising can only have a Sagittarian MC, but in the southern hemisphere, it is just possible for those born with very early Pisces rising to have a Scorpio MC. The MC can show the signs that we get on with best.

Pisces/Scorpio

This extremely unusual combination makes you very psychic indeed, to the point where it's almost inevitable that you will become involved in spiritualism, ghost hunting, spiritual healing, crystal healing, psychic art or something similar. You long to see beyond the veil and to commune with the gods. It's possible that the same spiritual impulse could take you into the world of religion or perhaps of Wicca. You may work in the health area, either as a doctor, nurse or midwife or as a therapist - either within the establishment, as in something like osteopathy, podiatry or as a complementary therapist of some kind. If Wicca interests you, herbalism might become your route to career fulfilment. You may choose to work in a prison, a mental hospital or any place where the most disadvantaged people gather to find help. You may go abroad to work in a war zone or to help orphans in Africa or some such thing.

Pisces/Sagittarius

The northern hemisphere, and in most southern hemisphere births, the MC is in Sagittarius. In this case, you may be attracted to the Sagittarian careers of teaching and training or the Piscean ones of social and medical work. Both signs have a strong urge to belong to organisations that help people so you may be drawn to work in a prison, a hospital, a mental hospital or a home for elderly or disabled people. Your desire to help and care could take you into childcare or nursing, while the Piscean attachment to feet could lead to a career in chiropody. Many Piscean subjects make a career out of caring for animals. You may take up voluntary work, possibly attached to a hospital. Your strong sense of justice could lead you into legal work or a career in arbitration. You may be very creative and artistic, so you may take up a job in the arts or have an important artistic hobby. Its possible that you take up a career an actor, musician, singer or dancer.

Both Pisces and Sagittarius are deeply interested in religion and philosophy, so this will figure strongly in your life. You may become involved in some kind of organised religion or take an interest in spiritual and mediumistic work and spiritual healing. You could take up this kind of work on either a full or a part-time basis. Angels and other mystical matters would appeal to you.

You are restless and you may be drawn to a job that involves rivers, lakes or the sea. Your talent for languages, combined with your itchy feet, may take you travelling around the world, either in connection with your work or as a hobby. Your restless nature is best suited to a job that involves being on the move rather than sitting in one place. You may work from home on some kind of private project, travelling out for purposes of research or observation. You may have a peculiar kind of love/hate relationship with motorcars, so if this affects you, you may be an excellent driver or you may never bother to learn.

The Descendant

The descendant, or the cusp of the seventh house, is traditionally supposed to show the type of person to whom we are most attracted. In the case of Pisces rising, the descendant is in Virgo. You look after your partner very well, and you will put up with a good deal of restriction or even unpleasantness. You cope with this by switching off and letting your mind roam elsewhere, away from the reality of your day-to-day life. If you are lucky, you will be able to find someone reliable, competent, hard working and decent. You may marry initially for security or in order to escape from your parents, but if you make a mistake the first time around, you will then look for someone who shares your interests, and who is willing to communicate with you and also offer you a peaceful, decent home life.

Love and Relating

Pisces is a very sexy sign, so if you have the right partner, this aspect of life becomes a major joy and pleasure for both of you. However, you may live for years with a poor lover. You need to give and receive love and affection, possibly because you were deprived of it when you were a child. Some of you divert your sex-drive into a calling, such as religion or good works. Your partner must be able to cope with your moodiness though.

Health

Traditionally, you are supposed to have bad feet, and it's often the case that your feet do give you problems. They are very sensitive and are apt to swell up when you are overtired or overworked. Your lungs and heart may be weak, as may be your spine. Females tend to suffer from menstrual problems, while both sexes will have difficulty in balancing their body fluids. This may result in high blood pressure, cystitis, varicose veins and a host of other problems. You may have something serious to contend with, such as epilepsy or some form of paralysis, but despite your poor health, you usually manage to live a full and long life.

Additional Information

☆ You love your home and you love to spend time in it, but you also love to travel and have holidays in the sun.

☆ You may never be wealthy, but you always have enough money for your needs.

☆ Pisces anywhere on a chart can show a link to alcoholism, so this may be your problem or it may afflict someone close to you.

☆ Where children are concerned, you will go to great lengths to ensure their happiness and to do whatever you can to make them successful. You may not have much to give them, but you will encourage them every step of the way. You really love your children, and when it comes to grandchildren, you simply adore them. You are very gentle and loving towards animals, babies and anything or anyone who is helpless.

☆ You may be a great salesperson, as your sign is associated with dreams, so you can sell the idea of a perfect holiday, a car that raises its owners status or a beauty makeover that's guaranteed to make an ordinary person look fabulous.

☆ You have to have a dream to keep you going, so that you don't descend into escapism through drink or drugs.

☆ Your only real drawbacks are your tendency to moodiness, your habit of taking offence when none is intended, and a tendency to ridicule others, or to go out of your way to offend them. Curb these habits if you want love and companionship in later life.

Pisces Rising Celebrities

Bob Monkhouse
Ringo Starr
Pauline Collins
Whitney Houston
Mark Knopfler
Dean Martin

16

Quick Clues to the Rising Signs

RISING SIGN	NATURE
Aries	Quiet voice, needs adventure, works in big organisations helping the public. Generous.
Taurus	Pleasant outer manner and good socially. Can be argumentative, obstinate, materialistic.
Gemini	Friendly, quick, clever, talkative, busy. Bad teeth, fine hair. Unhappy childhood leads to lack of confidence later.
Cancer	Slow moving, good salesperson, friendly. Either very good or very bad relationship with parents.
Leo	Great hair that looks interesting, vain, tough in business. Only really interested in self and own family.
Virgo	Unhappy childhood, much emphasis on appearing to do the right thing. Loud, can be difficult, obstinate. Own worst enemy.
Libra	Attractive, pleasant, sociable, lazy, fond of the good life. Artistic and musical. Marries when young.
Scorpio	Much resentment at things from childhood. Makes the best of difficulties and becomes a success later in life.
Sagittarius	Good looking with a nice smile. Quick, clever, but may flit from one job or person to another.
Capricorn	Hard circumstances in childhood, does quite well later, despite lingering health problem. Must guard against stinginess.
Aquarius	Had unusual parents or school experience, makes friends easily, nice smile; can be very successful once the right way is found.
Pisces	Either kind and friendly or hard and hostile. After difficult teens and twenties, does well in life. Loves children and grandchildren.

17

The Midheaven

The midheaven (MC) is so heavily influenced by the Asc that I think it's worth taking a slightly deeper look at it here.

Techie Data
Briefly, the MC is the point of intersection between the ecliptic and the meridian in a person's natal chart. If you would like a more detailed explanation, an Internet search will bring up a goodly number of references for you.

At the time of the spring and autumn equinoxes (21st March and 21st September), the days and the nights are more or less of equal length everywhere in the world. For births at these times of the year, the MC/IC line is nearer to perpendicular to the Asc/Dsc line, albeit with variance according to the birth latitude.

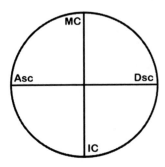

At the time of the solstices (21st June and 21st December), the MC/IC line can be at a steep angle to the Asc/Dsc line, as per the illustrations overleaf.

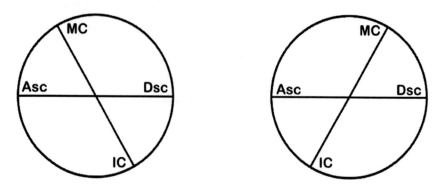

While the Asc tracks its way through a particular sign, the MC will also move along, but at some times of the year and in some latitudes, the angle that you can see in the illustrations can change rapidly.

Some rising signs take longer to rise than others, depending on the latitude and the time of year. In some cases, therefore, the sign takes so long to rise that the MC passes through two signs, and it may even touch a third. For example, Cancer rising can just touch on three MC signs. Southern hemisphere births can show the same effect, but in reverse, with Capricorn rising having three possible MCs.

Various MCs

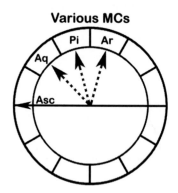

The Astrology of the MC

The MC is much underrated by astrologers. It has a more profound influence on the personality than we give it credit for, and it modifies the action of the rising sign far more than we realise. The MC and the tenth house represent the role we wish to play, what we want to become, and what we want to do with our lives. For instance, do we want to be seen as a respectable member of society, a doctor, teacher, writer, good mother, great gardener or what? This part of the horoscope operates on a surprisingly deep psychological level.

The MC is usually more concerned with activities and interests outside the home and family than within it, so astrologers often use it as a career indicator. It is certainly that, but it really relates to the person's true interests, which may have nothing to do with the way he earns his living. An example would be of a bus driver who is a keen ballroom dancer. He invests most of his time, attention, thought, energy and money into dancing, and only puts the minimum amount of thought into moving his bus around the neighbourhood.

While one can say that the MC is usually more interested in creating a possible future than delving into the past, even that isn't always the case. Take a Cancerian MC and Capricorn IC. This person may be the child of a real captain of industry, but he could well decide to turn away from his father's achievements and become a good family man instead. He may also be interested in history, the past, patriotism and things of the past, such as antiques, old clothes and old coins. This is a good illustration of where one comes from (the IC) and where one strives to get to (the MC). Moreover, when looking at the MC, you need to look at the houses nearby and the planets therein.

Although there is no hard and fast rule, the Asc often rules the way we present ourselves to others, especially those who we meet for the first time, while the MC (along with the Moon and other things) shows what we want to achieve or become. This means that two or three people with the same rising sign may have very different inner motivations if their MCs are in different signs. For example, a subject with Taurus rising should be extremely practical - so much so, that the subject may have no use for astrology, religion or any kind of philosophical or abstract concept. When this fixed/earth ascendant is accompanied by the equally practical and hard-headed cardinal/earth Capricorn MC, we are looking at a strong will, ambition, and a desire for a nice job in banking, complete with fat bonuses.

In a few cases, Taurus rising can be accompanied by an Aquarius MC, and that's a very different kettle of fish. While still practical and capable, this subject has values and interests in things that don't necessarily make money. He or she may be interested in saving the planet, saving animals or doing something for humanity. He may have a job that pays the mortgage alongside personal interests that are very different, and he may not advertise these to his work colleagues. Taurus rising folk *look* conservative, but one may be a member of the Conservative party, while the other works for Greenpeace.

There are people whose Sun sign and planetary positions make them appear extremely stable and sensible on the outside, but who are actually extremely moody and difficult. These subjects can switch from one thing to another in the blink of an eye. Look for water signs on both the Asc and MC. A classic example would be Cancer rising and Pisces on the MC. These people have moods that change with the tides, as they can be kind-hearted, humourous and friendly when they are in the right mood and then sharp tongued and hurtful when their mood changes.

Look at the element and quality of both the Asc and MC. If there is something in common, the outside manner and inner drives will have some similarity. A Scorpio Asc and Leo MC is made up of water and fire elements, but these are both fixed signs, and Leo is less emotional than Scorpio. Now look at Scorpio rising with a Virgo MC. Scorpio is fixed/water and Virgo is mutable/earth, and somehow this combination finds it hard to keep its feet on the ground. I've known several people with this combination, and while they were all intelligent and charming, a number of them had problems with drugs and alcohol. It appears that the mutable Virgo MC and the escapist Pisces IC can't give the determined, obstinate, moody and emotional Scorpio Asc the strength it needs. To quote my friend Jon Dee, the situation is like a tree that looks good but whose roots and trunk aren't strong enough to support the canopy. Needless to say, if other planets in the chart offer strength, then the situation is much improved, and the problems can be overcome.

The double cardinal Libra Asc with Cancer MC emphasises cardinality. Cardinality wants its own way at all costs, and with the addition of moody, emotional Cancer, the famous Libran logic turns into arguments and scenes. A Libra Asc and Leo MC combo is less hysterical, partly because Leo is far less emotional than Cancer. In addition, this subject will find an outlet for his or her talent and determination in music, the arts, show business or arbitration. The stress in the chart is relieved because the subject finds something to get his teeth into.

One final point worth mentioning is that marriages and partnerships where one person has the Sun on the other's MC tend to work well. If both parties have this connection, the marriage should be extremely successful.

If all this isn't enough, look into the Decans and Dwaads of the MC as well. These have only a short chapter here, because they are beyond the scope of this book, but as usual, an Internet search will find a number of references. These interesting astrological features are also fully explained in my book, 'The Hidden Zodiac'.

Quick Guide to the Midheaven

I've given a very full explanation of the MC in this book, along with a description of each Asc/MC combination within each rising sign chapter, but here is a short guide for easy reference.

Aries MC

These individuals are imbued with a powerful instinct for self-preservation and a strong urge to serve their own interests. They are independent folk who don't allow others to take advantage of them, but while they make very pleasant and amusing acquaintances, they are not easy to live or work with. They work best when self-employed or in the tough world of high-level politics. They are competitive.

Taurus MC

These people seek stability, wealth and comfort, looking forward to the day when their mortgage is paid up and when they can own a farm or have nice things. These individuals have strong wills, and they can carry things through to a conclusion. They find a job that they like and stick with it. They know how to relax and enjoy life so they don't get too stressed out.

Gemini MC

It can be hard for these folk to stick to one job, because they get bored very quickly, so they need variety, changes of scene and new faces at intervals. Teaching is a good option for these people, but they are unlikely to stay in one job for more than a couple of years at a time. These subjects are probably the most caring and protective of their families of any astrological type.

Cancer MC

These subjects can make a career out of household tasks, such as catering, selling furniture, estate agency work, painting and decorating or perhaps something linked to the past, such as antique and stamp collecting. They remain close to their families throughout life and they may work from home or have a small business where family members to join in and take part in the work.

Leo MC

There is a touch of show-business about these people, so they may spend some of their time engaged in music, dancing or the world of art, either as a job or as a sideline. They like to work in glamourous or highly respected fields and they usually reach the top of the ladder. When they fall in love, it is deep and very real, but they may love their children and pets more than their partners.

Virgo MC

Many of these people work in the fields of health, healing or psychology. Some love on new technology, while others hate it, and some are good at detailed work, such as design and dressmaking. They all seem to dislike doing accounts and figure work. These folk are close to their families, especially their fathers, even though they argue with them from time to time.

Libra MC

This MC leads to an interest in arbitration, trades union or legal work, and it can also lead to a successful career in teaching. These folk are friendly, sociable, sometimes very sophisticated, elegant, attractive and well travelled. Many of them are somewhat interested in astrology and spiritual matters. While too restless and argumentative for family life, they do love their children.

Scorpio MC

These people are keen on business, and their ability to persuade others can make them good salespeople. They need to have a house that is paid for, a bit of land and nice things. While they value family life, they also need freedom to come and go, as they travel for fun and on business. They are either very generous or extremely stingy. There are no half measures with these folk.

Sagittarius MC

This is a lucky MC, so these people get themselves out of difficulties and fall on their feet even in times of trouble. They are likely to travel in connection with work or for pleasure. They may be eccentric and exotic or ultra conservative, but they like to be stylish and modern. Their quick minds can take them to the pinnacle of power and influence, as long as they don't get distracted by family demands.

Capricorn MC

This MC confers executive ability and ambition but it can make these people too devoted to money and success for a balanced life, so they may be too serious. They may not be quick at what they do but they are very thorough. On the plus side, they love music, singing, dancing and art, and they enjoy hobbies in these areas. They also enjoy socialising either as part of their work or as a change from it.

Aquarius MC

These people are hard to influence but they love to explore ideas and they will accept something, when they can prove to themselves that it works. They need an interesting career but they may have two part time jobs on the go at once to give them variety. Money is less important than new ideas, especially idealistic ones. They love new technology and will use any excuse to buy a new gadget. These people may be too cool to adapt well to family life.

Pisces MC

These people take jobs with travel or where they deal with the general public. They are excellent salespeople, and reliable workers who are clever at solving problems. At home, they are less pleasant, as they are apt to be moody - sometimes kind and loving, but then spiteful and hurtful, or silent and sulky. They need a partner who is insensitive and self-absorbed. They may suffer from health problems or have family members who are sick.

18

The Immum Coeli

The IC is at the bottom of the birthchart, directly opposite to the midheaven, and it concerns the private side of life, including the home and the family. Traditionally, the IC also refers to the beginning and ending of one's life, the mother or mother figure, the background to anything, and any kind of ancestral memory.

The IC is traditionally associated with the mother, but it can relate to any person or any circumstance that influenced the person's past. As a perfect illustration, I give you the following true story, as related by my best friend, Jon Dee. It's a real classic…

'I was doing a chart for this bloke when I spotted an afflicted Neptune in his fourth house, close to the IC. Being in a whimsical mood at the time, and knowing that the guy came from the port city of Liverpool, I asked him whether his father had been a drunken sailor. My client thought for a moment and then replied, "No, my dad was a drunken swimming pool attendant!"'

As the IC, like the Asc, also relates so much to childhood influences, I've gone into it here, sign by sign.

Aries IC

There may have been a conflict going on in the family at the time you were born. However, your childhood environment was cheerful and your parents helpful and encouraging. Your adult home is an open and friendly place with many visitors and a lot of fun and noise. You could fill your home with gadgets or sports equipment.

Taurus IC

Your birth should have been comfortable and well arranged, and if your early environment was lacking in either material or emotional comforts, you can rest assured that your later life will make up for this. Your own adult home will be full of music and beauty, and probably over-furnished and full of souvenirs.

Gemini IC

This sign suggests a strange start in life, possibly due to some kind of disruption in your family or in your schooling. You will probably be active and working right up to the end of your days. You will have either exceptionally good or exceptionally bad relationships with your brothers and sisters. Your own adult home will be full of books, music and people, and you may run some kind of business from it. You need freedom to come and go, but the home you return to will be spacious and full of expensive furniture and equipment.

Cancer IC

Your early experiences will have a strong impact on your future development. You should remain close to your parents throughout their lives. Your adult home will be very important to you and even though you frequently travel away from it, you see it as a safe haven. You may work partially or wholly from your home. You may enjoy cooking, and your kitchen should be very well equipped. You could collect odds and ends, antiques or even junk.

Leo IC

Your early days could have been very difficult, either because you were over-disciplined or because your parents lived a nomadic existence. Later on, you try to make a traditional and comfortable home, but this may become disrupted in some way. You may want a nice home, but somehow find that you are prevented from spending a lot of money on it. If you entertain, you will do so in style and if you work from home, you will make sure that you have all the latest equipment to hand.

Virgo IC

Your early life could have been difficult, either in the home or at school. However, your home environment was full of books and music. Your parents would have placed a bit too much importance on good behaviour, a proper diet and cleanliness, and too little on how you felt. Your adult home is spacious and comfortable, with a well-stocked kitchen. If you work from home, you will have all the latest communications equipment.

Libra IC

Your early life would have been calm, pleasant and loving, with nice surroundings and respectable parents. Your adult home should be large and very comfortable, full of artistic objects and music. You probably like cooking, so your kitchen will be well equipped, but any entertaining that you do will be on a small scale.

Scorpio IC

The circumstances of your birth may have been strange, and there could have been some kind of conflict raging in the family at the time you were born. The atmosphere in your childhood home may have been tense and uncomfortable. Your adult home would be far more pleasant, with an emphasis on good food and a comfortable lifestyle, but you must guard against tension creeping in even there. You may find that you spend a good deal of time alone in your home, either by choice or by circumstances.

Sagittarius IC

Your early life may have been peculiar, either because your parents were heavily involved in religious activities or because they were immigrants from another culture. You may have lived in two worlds at the same time, or moved from one country to another and possibly back to the first again. Your adult home will be pleasant and open, not over-tidy but full of interesting knick-knacks. You may work from home or use it as a base.

Capricorn IC

Your childhood home may have been happy, although lacking in material comforts, or it may have been a source of tension and stress. You would have been encouraged to work hard for material success. Your latter days will be very comfortable and you could well end up being very rich. Your adult home will be well organised and filled with valuable goods, but you may decide to keep animals in preference to having children.

Aquarius IC

During childhood, your life at home or school may have been very unsettled or even eccentric. Your adult home might be sumptuous and filled with expensive goods and gadgets or filled with an odd assortment of junk. Alternatively, your furniture and equipment could be ultra modern. You may work from your home part of the time. Your home is often filled with friends and neighbours. You may move house a lot.

Pisces IC

There may have been some mystery surrounding the circumstances of your birth or alternatively, you might have been brought up in a nomadic family. Both your childhood home and your later adult one will reflect the many interests of the people who live in it. These may include books and equipment associated with the occult, magic, religion or travel. Your surroundings may have been unconventional, perhaps arty or musical. Your children will have a good deal of freedom, but they may not actually communicate much with you.

19

The Descendant

The Descendant can indicate the virtues and values that we find attractive in others, and many of us are drawn to those people whose Sun or Moon is in their Dsc sign. My observations over the years show that we find more friends than lovers in this sign.

DESCENDANT	ATTRIBUTES
Aries	You seek adventurous, active, fun friends
Taurus	You choose stable, reliable and well-off friends.
Gemini	You want friends for fun and conversation.
Cancer	Perhaps you seek motherly friends.
Leo	Your choose lively, fashionable and sophisticated friends.
Virgo	You value competent, efficient colleagues.
Libra	Intelligent friends who share your mental wavelength suit you.
Scorpio	Shared interests and mutual respect are important.
Sagittarius	You need friends who enjoy a good laugh.
Capricorn	Your friends are few, but valued, and probably older.
Aquarius	You have lots of friends, and you love to chat with them.
Pisces	Your friends must share your interests.

20

The Cusps

A cusp is the point where one sign ends and the next begins, so if your Sun or ascendant is on a cusp, these may be the results:

Aries/Taurus cusp

This belongs to a powerful personality with the kind of vision that allows the individual to look forward while retaining strong links to the past. This person can be charming when he feels like it, but also determined, obstinate and possibly aggressive. There is a strong sexual drive that may or may not be diverted into other activities. The person is probably interested in art, music or architecture and he or she could be a powerful, visionary leader, or a complete mess.

Taurus/Gemini cusp

This person can be a creative dreamer, a self-indulgent person who wants the good life and who may even make an effort to work for it if pressed. The subject is dexterous and good at do-it-yourself or engineering. This person likes travel, and enjoys work and family life. He may move and talk slowly, but the mind is quick and shrewd.

Gemini/Cancer cusp

This person is moody and difficult to understand, but the subject is a good listener and a good talker. He could be a good accountant or business person. Although desperate for a good relationship, this confusing person is both a mixer and a loner. The subject may always be on the move, looking for the most advantageous mixture of circumstances. He is sensitive and easily hurt.

Cancer/Leo cusp

This subject wants to make a splash, to be noticed and respected, but he may be too lazy to achieve this ambition, so he may try to marry someone who has a good income instead. The native is probably quite artistic and certainly creative, with a talent for working in the financial field, and may be an excellent accountant or insurance salesman. May be an excellent sales person.

Leo/Virgo cusp

A nervy, high achiever who never thinks he has done enough. He can become ill when things go wrong or he can punish himself unnecessarily. Emotionally vulnerable, slow to grow up or accept change, he needs to gain confidence. He also needs a stable family life. He is kind hearted and good to family and friends, but he can be moody and unpleasant at times.

Virgo/Libra cusp

This subject is highly sexed and highly charged with many other kinds of energy as well. He enjoys work, especially if it gives him a chance to manage others, and he may travel extensively in connection with his work. The subject has many secrets to keep, and though fascinating, he or she is not easy to live with. This subject may dabble at things rather than do things thoroughly.

Libra/Scorpio cusp

This person's spine and legs may be affected in some way, even to the point of semi-paralysis. Despite any disability, the subject overcomes everything and goes on to have an interesting career. Marriage and other family or close relationships are likely to be excellent, but there may be no children. The outer manner may be abrupt, so the subject needs to work on this.

Scorpio/Sagittarius cusp

Here, we have a mystical or spiritual outlook, with a strong desire to help others. This person suffers more than most and puts up with it for longer than is necessary. This is a reliable and hard worker who will stick to a job until the finish, but he likes variety in a job and is happy to travel for business. This subject can suffer from accidents to the legs, but seems to overcome everything and keep going. He may be drawn to work in the fields of medicine or religion.

Sagittarius/Capricorn cusp

This subject is fascinated by the occult and may be very psychic. This person can be businesslike one minute, but unrealistic the next. He needs to relax and have fun, as all work and no play makes him dull. Family and friends depend on the subject, but don't give much back in return. He must guard against being abrupt or offensive.

Capricorn/Aquarius cusp

Outwardly competent and often sarcastic to the point of being offensive, but at the same time idealistic and kind hearted, this person is very good to his family and close friends, but may be too involved with work to spend much time with them. This subject judges him or herself by work or status rather than as a person. Muddle-headed and somewhat messy administratively, he is at his best when teaching or helping others. This person's ideas are often very clever and truly workable.

Aquarius/Pisces cusp

Here is a strange mixture of weirdness and shrewdness, with leanings towards astrology and psychism. He or she can inspire others with vision, but daily life may be chaotic. This person may be very eccentric and faddy about everything, from food to clothing and the household. He may prefer animals to people.

Pisces/Aries cusp

This person may choose to work in the astrological or psychic world. The mixture of superb intuition coupled with commercial instincts can make this subject very successful in almost any field of endeavour. However, his or her high ideals, soapbox or absorbing interests can make the individual hard to live with. A good sales person and a clever politician.

21

The Decans

Each sign of the zodiac is divided into thirty degrees, and further broken down into three groups of ten degrees; these sub-sections are called decans. The first decan is sub-ruled by its own sign, the second is sub-ruled by the next sign of the same element, and the third decan is sub-ruled by the remaining sign in that element.

For example, the sign of Aquarius is an air sign. The first decan is sub-ruled by Aquarius itself, the second by Gemini because it's the next air sign round the zodiac system, and the third decan is sub-ruled by Libra. If you are into astrology enough to know the degree of your ascendant, you can easily work out which decan was rising. The first decan is found anywhere from 0 degrees of a sign to 9 deg 59 min of the sign; the second decan is from 10 degrees to 19 deg.59 min, and the third decan at 20 degrees to 29 deg.59 min.

The decans subtly modify the influence of the rising sign, but they can also demonstrate links to other members of the family. For instance, I've come across one mother and her children who link like this:

Mother: Sun Cancer in the Scorpio decan, rising sign Scorpio in the Cancer decan.
Son: Sun Scorpio in the Cancer decan, rising sign Cancer in the Scorpio decan.
Daughter: Moon Scorpio in the Cancer decan, rising sign Cancer in the Scorpio decan.

Here is a very brief introduction to the influence of the decans. If you want to know more about this fascinating subject, treat yourself to a copy of my book 'The Hidden Zodiac', as it's all about the Decans, and Dwaads as well.

Sign and Decan	Influence
Aries/Aries	A real go-getter, likely to lack consideration for others.
Aries/Leo	A go-getter who finishes what he starts.
Aries/Sagittarius	Many interests, good teacher.
Taurus/Taurus	Very capable, but too obstinate.
Taurus/Virgo	A good worker, good with details.
Taurus/Capricorn	An excellent banker or businessperson.
Gemini/Gemini	A flirt, very clever, a good memory.
Gemini/Libra	Good team worker, but may be argumentative.
Gemini/Aquarius	Clever, but a deeper and more serious mind.
Cancer/Cancer	Very attached to family, loves travel.
Cancer/Scorpio	Loves travel, chooses a weak partner to mother.
Cancer/Pisces	Intuitive, spiritual, can be moody.
Leo/Leo	Very enterprising and successful.
Leo/Sagittarius	Loves travel and philosophy.
Leo/Aries	Enterprising, will follow a hunch in business.
Virgo/Virgo	Reliable worker, but neurotic.
Virgo/Capricorn	Good business head, but might be cold hearted.
Virgo/Taurus	Clever at design and construction.

Sign and Decan	Influence
Libra/Libra	Attractive, lazy, argumentative.
Libra/Aquarius	Good ideas, but may be impractical.
Libra/Gemini	Good in business, health may be poor.
Scorpio/Scorpio	Likes business, but emotions dominate thinking.
Scorpio/Pisces	Intuitive, psychic, may be stingy in small ways.
Scorpio/Cancer	Loves home, family, friends, work and travel.
Sagittarius/Sagittarius	Adventurous, interested in everything.
Sagittarius/Aries	Hot tempered, sometimes acts without thinking.
Sagittarius/Leo	Steady and able to achieve and reach goals.
Capricorn/Capricorn	Can be workaholic, otherwise very status conscious.
Capricorn/Taurus	Practical, sensible, good homemaker.
Capricorn/Virgo	Clever business person, good accountant.
Aquarius/Aquarius	Very clever, but impractical ideas and soapbox mentality.
Aquarius/Gemini	Bright, humourous, good with figure work.
Aquarius/Libra	Laid back, great ideas, but nothing may come of them.
Pisces/Pisces	Very dreamy, artistic, may live chaotic lifestyle.
Pisces/Cancer	Good at business, sales and with people, but stingy.
Pisces/Scorpio	Can be over-emotional and act without thinking.

22

Rising Planets

The term rising planet refers to a planet in the first or second house that will rise above the ascendant within a few hours of a child's birth. The range has broadened a little now to include a planet in the twelfth house that has already risen, as long as it's close to the ascendant. If there is only one planet near the ascendant, it will be strongly emphasised. If there is a group of planets, then the house and the sign that it occupies will be stressed. A rising planet can be almost as important as the Sun in a birthchart.

In astro-cartography (ACG) (also known as locational astrology), planets close to the ascendant at the time of birth can be considered as having moved away from it, if the person moves to another part of the world. If you want to learn more about ACG, there are just a few books available on the subject, one of which is Martin Davis's excellent book, 'Astrolocality Astrology'. Other ACG authors to look for are Erin Sullivan and Jim Lewis. I have also written a book on the subject, called 'Astrology on the Move'.

Sun Conjunct Ascendant

If the Sun and the ascendant are in the same sign, the sign becomes an ultra important factor on the chart. If the Sun and ascendant were in adjoining signs (e.g. Sun in Libra, Virgo rising), both signs would be emphasised, but not as much. Transits and progressions over that part of the chart will be exceptionally noticeable. If the two factors are in the same sign, there is no need for the ascendant to act as a shield to the personality. The Sun's influence makes for a confident, outgoing, well-integrated person who was encouraged and loved in childhood. If the Asc is a difficult one (Virgo, Capricorn or Gemini for instance), the childhood was hard, but the subject had the inner strength to rise above the problems, and he or she achieve a good deal of success in spite of them - or maybe because of them.

These powerful personalities need to express themselves in daily life, and they put their own stamp on everything. They cannot live or work in a subservient position. They are strong and healthy, with good powers of recovery from illness, despite potential problems in connection with the back or heart. These people are initiators who are not happy to be in the hands of others or the hands of fate, and they turn all situations to their own advantage. They have sunny personalities, but they can be arrogant.

Moon Conjunct Ascendant

This placement denotes a sensitive and vulnerable nature. The feelings are close to the surface and are easily brought into play. The subject reacts in an intensely personal way to every stimulus and he links easily to the feelings of others. The mother may be an extremely powerful (and possibly extraordinary) figure, and her life and emotions will have a profound effect. The subject will remain close to her, perhaps remaining involved in her life and her work for many years. It's possible that the subject can 'remember' things that happened to his mother while he was in the womb! Childhood experiences and early training remain in the subject's unconscious throughout his life. He or she is likely to be the eldest sibling in a family.

There is a strong need to create a home and family as well as to look after others by working in one of the caring professions. These subjects want to protect the environment, preserve places, buildings and objects from the past and create a better, kinder and safer future for mankind. Psychic ability is almost always present, and there may even be vestigial memories of previous lives. All forms of intuition are well developed. These people love travel and to be on or by water. They also like to run a small business for themselves. They are interested in history and tradition and they may try to revive traditional crafts, or collect fine things from the past. They retreat from the rat race from time to time, in order to calm themselves and recharge their emotional batteries. Oddly enough, the Moon is associated with work in the public eye, or for the public good, so these people often become well-known personalities. Being sensitive, they become depressed or downhearted and they may absorb the unhappiness of others; this psychic absorption can make them ill. In a notably macho or materialistic chart, this Moon placement lends introspection and sensitivity to the needs and feelings of others.

Mercury Conjunct Ascendant

Mercury is concerned with communication and the mentality, therefore these subjects are fluent talkers and good communicators. They range from highly intelligent to bright, active, sensible and street-wise. They work in careers directly involved with people and with communications. These people have good minds, but they may never make much use of their brains. They switch off from time to time, to allow the mind to relax. They are dutiful towards parents and either very close to siblings or at odds with them. They are happiest working for themselves or in their own little department, and they need to feel that their work is appreciated. They can be restless, easily bored, interesting to listen to, humourous and sometimes very sarcastic. Their health is not good, but they can also be hypochondriacs in some instances. In a stodgy or over-practical chart, this Mercury placement adds quickness of mind, curiosity and adaptability.

Venus Conjunct Ascendant

This confers good looks and a pleasant social manner, with a pleasant speaking voice, and possibly a good singing voice. These subjects are refined and they dislike anything ugly, dirty or vulgar. They take jobs where they can create beauty in some way, for example as a gardener, furniture designer, artist, hairdresser or dancer. Alternatively, they take up artistic or attractive hobbies. They can be good arbitrators, with a natural desire to create harmony and understanding. They can also be diplomats and ambassadors who use their charm and tact in their daily lives.

These people enjoy making money and spending it on attractive and valuable goods. They are concerned about values, both in terms of getting value for money and in terms of personal values and priorities. They won't sacrifice anything they value for the sake of others. They can be sleepy and lazy or argumentative in some cases. Venus on the ascendant can add placidity and pleasantness to an otherwise forceful, dynamic or neurotic chart.

Mars Conjunct Ascendant

This adds impulsiveness, enterprise, courage and a quick temper. These people make things happen where other less courageous souls would prefer to run away and hide. They stand out in a crowd, dominating those around them. They can become highly successful achievers, who are best suited for positions of leadership or as self-employed entrepreneurs. Successful sports people tend to have this Mars placement, because above all, it's associated with competitiveness. In an otherwise timid, stodgy or lazy chart, this can add enterprise, enthusiasm, energy and will power. The person's birth may have been fraught with danger, or the prevailing situation may have been dangerous.

Jupiter Conjunct Ascendant

These people are attractive, with sunny smiles and good teeth. This placement adds the kind of broad frame and comfortable shape that looks great on a man, but that's unfashionable nowadays for a woman. The outer manner is cheerful, optimistic and confident, and these people carry authority well and can be inspirational leaders. These subjects are unlikely to be biased against any class or colour of person and they are not the slightest bit snobbish, but they can be intolerant of wannabes and posers. This placement gives a love of travel and exploration, plus a touch of studiousness, and these people may be interested in philosophy and metaphysical subjects. They may be lucky gamblers, especially on horses. Their minds are good and they can usually see both sides of any argument, but they can also become very attached to their own opinions. I've noticed that people who have this planet rising experience quite drastic ups and downs where money is concerned.

They are invariably attractive, but the optimism which the old time astrologers associate with this planet can be dampened if there is a good deal of water on the chart. Nevertheless, this placement adds a touch of enterprise, luck and vision to an otherwise stodgy or earthbound chart. Jupiter rising subjects travel widely, often in connection with their work, and some eventually leave their country of origin altogether.

Saturn Conjunct Ascendant

These people are squashed in childhood so that they don't develop much confidence or self-worth, but they can become surprisingly successful later in life, due perhaps to their tendency to put their noses to the grindstone and keep them there. This planet brings insecurity and even fear during childhood. These subjects may have lost parents and been brought up by grandparents, or other older people who may have taken them in on sufferance. If the home life were all right, school would have been a nightmare. These types are happy to grow up, because that's when life starts to improve.

Hiding their real needs and feelings, they may even deny themselves the right to have any needs other than those which other people consider suitable. Their natural creativity may be squashed because it doesn't fit in with the requirements of those around them. Depending upon the rest of the chart, this childhood can develop a hard and aggressive attitude to others later in life. Alternatively, these people may become doormats who avoid making even reasonable demands upon others. In a way, this is not such a bad thing, as these people are very independent and they neither lean on nor drain the energy of others. Some rise above the unpromising start and become outstanding success stories. These subjects take commitments very seriously and they finish what they start. Many of them become writers or work in publishing, where patience and attention to details are important. They also have a talent for maths and science. They may be religious, but they tend to be realistic and down-to-earth as well.

Saturn on the ascendant or in opposition or square to it at the time of birth indicates a difficult birth. Another interesting theory is that the parents worked hard while the child was young, giving him especially diligent parental role models. They may be deaf or suffer with some chronic ailment.

Uranus Conjunct Ascendant

These individuals may be idealistic, unpredictable and quite fascinating. Their interests are unusual, they are highly intuitive and able to jump to the right conclusion and they may be into astrology and psychic matters. Humanitarian and broad-minded, these people opt for an unusual way of life, either following unusual beliefs or making them up as they go along. Their lives take peculiar twists and turns, partly because they are prey to unusual circumstances and partly because they can't stand too much normality. These individuals are clever, but they can also be obstinate. They have good minds that are directed towards unusual subjects. They may be cranky, strange or visionary, whilst at the same time being stubborn and determined. Even an extremely mundane chart will be enlivened by this placement.

Neptune Conjunct Ascendant

This fascinating planet can make people into inspired artists, glamourous film stars or complete nut cases – or all three. The childhood may have been strange, and there could have been some kind of mystery surrounding birth and parentage. It's possible that one or more of the parents were absent or very peculiar, even to the extent of being mentally ill. These subjects are sensitive, vulnerable and easily hurt, and they may never have a clear idea of their own needs and feelings, trying to live to the rules of others – only discovering later that these rules were abnormal or twisted in some way. This placement can make subjects psychic, mediumistic or prone to fantasies. Loneliness or isolation in childhood will have encouraged these children to read, think, dream and listen to music, and to develop their creativity and imagination. In extreme cases, they lose track of reality altogether. Bear in mind the rest of the chart when Neptune is rising, because if it's practical and sensible, this will simply add artistry and sensitivity rather than genuine lunacy.

These people may work in the photography, music or the psychic fields, and they have a soft spot for animals or those who are weak and vulnerable, so some work for charity organisations, while others collect lame ducks.

Pluto Conjunct Ascendant

These people want to control, direct and guide the lives of others, so they may go into politics. This directing instinct can take them into the world of medicine, the media or teaching. The personality is so controlled that it's hard to work out just what these people are thinking or what really motivates them. They may be pleasant at work and hard at home or vice versa. Others put them down when they are young, so they can be slow to grow up. They can have deep-seated resentments due to being made to feel inadequate at home or at school when young. They seek to overcome these feelings later in life, sometimes by being economical with the truth.

These subjects have sharp minds and the kind of insight that allow them to pick up even the mildest of undercurrents, and they always know when someone doesn't like them. They may appear mild, gentle and amenable, but when challenged or hurt, they lash out. This planet adds tenacity and reliability to the chart, so they don't take time off work when feeling off colour. They finish what they start, arrive in good time for appointments, and they are alert and properly equipped to do what is required. They must be able to come and go as they please. This planet adds sexuality, and depending upon circumstances and the rest of the chart, this may be an important issue. If this aspect of life is squashed, these subjects can become embittered or depressed.

The person may have been born into a family in mourning or at a time of danger, such as during a war. For example, bombs were falling while my mother was in labour with me, and Pluto rises in my chart!

Chiron Conjunct Ascendant

Chiron rising is rather like Saturn rising, in that the person will have severe problems during childhood, perhaps through illness or through being badly treated by those around him. This can lead these people to work in the fields of healing or psychology, where they use their own understanding of pain to help others.

North or South Node Conjunct Ascendant

When either node is conjunct the Asc, fame and fortune are possible.

23

Predictive Techniques

The ascendant may not have the impact of planetary transits and progressions, but it does have valuable uses, particularly when looking at a year in question and when judging long-term situations. I will show you the easiest, and probably the best method of judging the changes that a progressed ascendant can bring.

Degree For a Year Progressions
There are many ways to progress your Asc, but this is the easiest, as all it requires is that you move the Asc forward by a degree for each year of your life. There are 30 degrees within each sign, running from 0 to 29.

A person with an Asc at 12 degrees of Aries will see the Asc progress into Taurus at the age of seventeen, and onwards to Gemini at 47 and Cancer at the age of 77.

When an Asc is very early in a sign, that rising sign has more impact on the personality, partly because most of the first house is in that sign, but also because it will take several years before the Asc can progress to the next sign. Conversely, when an ascendant is very late in a sign, it may have less impact, because much of the first house is in the next sign along, and also because the progressed Asc will leave the rising sign and move into the next one in early childhood.

After considering the age at which the progressed Asc changes sign, you can look for the age at which it crosses another planet, as this will set off some kind of event, the nature of which depends upon the planet in question.

Aspects also work with this system, so if you are far enough into astrology to understand them, you can look back over your life to see what happened in a year when the progressed Asc made a sextile or trine to a planet or when it squared or opposed one. Remember to consider the nature of the planet in question. I give a brief rundown on each planet later in this chapter.

Other Forms of Progression

This section is for those of you who have some astrological knowledge.

☆ You can progress the MC by the rate at which it moves, and then reset the Asc appropriately.

☆ You can progress the Asc by the rate at which the Sun moves, thus using Solar Arc Directions.

☆ You can use Secondary Directions, which are also called Day-For-a-Year Progressions.

☆ Secondary Directions move the ascendant more slowly than the other methods, as long as you live in the same area throughout your life (say by remaining within sixty miles or so of your place of birth). It will move along slowly. If you move to another part of the country or another part of the world, the progressed Asc moves in strange ways, and it can even move back to an earlier position than it was at birth. For example, Jan was born in Zambia and he now lives in Plymouth, so his progressed Asc is actually a degree or two back from its position at birth.

Progressing the Midheaven

You may find the MC even more effective than the Asc as a tool for predicting events. Either progress the MC a degree for a year or select Secondary Directions on your computer software to locate a progressed MC position.

Degree for a year MC progressions are particularly useful when rectifying a birthchart, which means finding the Asc for someone who only has a vague idea of the time of birth, as you will see in the following chapter on rectification.

Transits

This is the first kind of predictive technique that all astrologers learn, and it involves using the ephemeris (book of tables) or an astrology program to locate the position of the planets in the sky at any one time. If you can link the figures in your book or on your computer screen to what you see in the sky, you can often go out at night and watch the lunar and planetary aspects looking down on you.

Check out any planets that cross the Asc, particularly those slow moving outer planets that transform our lives, such as Pluto, Neptune, Uranus and Saturn. Look at the aspects that planets make to the Asc as they work their way round your chart. You will find that the faster moving inner planets, such as the Moon, Mercury and Venus won't probably make much of an impact, other than a short lived one on the day that they cross the Asc. Aspects from the outer planets will make themselves felt, though.

ASPECT	DISTANCE	EFFECT
Conjunction	0 degrees	Both very good and very bad, depending upon the planet.
Semi-sextile	30 degrees	Mildly pleasant or mildly irritating.
Sextile	60 degrees	Beneficial.
Square	90 degrees	Difficult.
Trine	120 degrees	Beneficial.
Inconjunct	150 degrees	Awkward, tense, irritating.
Opposition	180 degrees	Can be good, but often difficult.

The Planets by Progression or Transit

This is a brief rundown of the way each planet behaves and the impact that it might have on the Asc by progression or transit.

PLANET	AREAS OF INFLUENCE
Sun	Happy time, luck, success, creative, children might become important now. If a difficult aspect, can feel like a long period of bad luck, illness, slipped discs, heart trouble.
Moon	Dealings with parents, family life, house move, renovations, starting a small business. Joy or sadness.
Mercury	Education, exams, replacing office equipment, getting job, cars, transport, travel, communications, neighbours and neighbourhood, health. Increased curiosity.
Venus	Love, relationships, harmony, social life, personal finances, personal purchases and possessions, abundance. Loss, extravagance, expense, trouble with love life, disharmony.
Mars	Drive, ambition, confidence when starting something new, sex, activity, fighting for what you want or for what is right. Attack, accidents, operations, fevers, sudden setbacks.
Jupiter	Expansion of horizons, legal matters, foreigners and travel, spiritual matters. Legal or financial trouble, over-expansion.
Saturn	Putting down roots, attention to details, thoroughness, a good job, a step up the ladder, a serious attitude, help from superiors or elders. Struggle, illness, setbacks, a dampening effect.
Uranus	Breakout and a fresh approach, originality, friends, groups and societies, modern ideas, astrology. Sudden setbacks, loss of friendship or loss of a group or club situation.
Neptune	Dreams come true, spiritual growth, artistry, music, the sea and pleasant interludes, kindness. Muddle, disillusion, swindles, not being able to see what's going on.
Pluto	Period of major transformation will be hard to live through, but will eventually lead to a better way of life. Death, birth, taxes, other people's money, shared resources, marriage and divorce, legacies, legal matters. Major events in life.
Chiron	Health and healing, accidents, illness, operations, transformation as a result of this. Interest in the healing arts and in music.

Not only People…

All the above ideas can be applied to a business, a property, a situation, a pet animal, a governmental administration or a national election. It could apply to a city, a country, a reign, or anything else that has a definite time, date and place of birth.

Retrograde Progressions

There are times when planets appear to go backwards in the sky, and this effect is called retrograde motion. The Moon and Sun are the only 'planets' that can never go retrograde. When a progressing planet crosses the ascendant, retrogrades back over it and then passes over it again by forward motion, matters that are symbolised by that planet become more obvious. During the retrograde period, these matters may be delayed or problematical but the final forward progression will clear away the problem and bring ultimate benefits.

When a planet makes this 'triple conjunction' by progression over the Asc, it will certainly make its presence felt. Only the inner planets of Mercury, Venus and Mars move quickly enough to do this during the average lifetime. The Outer planets move so slowly by progression that they sit in the same place for decades, so while their effects may be felt over the long term, they cannot bring sudden or unexpected changes.

Retrograde Transits

Where transiting planets are concerned, the inner planets move too quickly to be important, although an inner planet passing, retrograding and then re-passing the Asc will make its presence felt for a while. For instance, Mercury may pass the Asc, retrograde back over it a week or so later and then move forward over it again, marking a month or so of intense Mercurial activity. Venus will take a little longer to do this, and Mars will hang around in the vicinity of the Asc for several months, making its presence obvious while doing so.

Transits by outer planets are more important, so if they make this 'triple conjunction' to the Asc, this will mark an extended period in which the effects of the planet can be felt. Obviously, a planet such as Saturn or Pluto can bring difficulties, but even these planets have their good sides. The outcome for a 'triple conjunction' of Saturn to the Asc will be growth and consolidation, while Pluto will ultimately bring birth or rebirth, financial and business improvements and possibly an inheritance or money from a divorce settlement, after an extended period of aggravation. This planet can bring personal transformation and personal improvement, so that the person gets into shape, tosses out any old clothes and buys better ones, makes new friends, gets a better job, moves to a larger/smaller home, finds a soul-mate, discovers good sex and so on.

A Uranus 'triple conjunction' would bring a complete change of life and a totally new outlook. A Neptune situation would bring art, music or mystical events into the subject's life, and it might encourage a move to the seaside. Jupiter brings travel, new opportunities, a fresh outlook, perhaps also an interest in education, or success in exams.

24

Rectification

If you're interested in rectification, try my book, 'What Time Were You Born?', as it's helpful to those people looking for their own or someone else's time of birth.

If you have an approximate birth time, say for example between about 2:00 and 3:00, you need to make up a chart for 2:30 and then do a little fine-tuning. You do this by moving the midheaven slowly forwards. The MC moves at a degree for a year, therefore events can be pinpointed by the aspects it makes to other planets on the natal chart as it progresses. The subject can be asked to mention any particularly memorable events in his childhood and the rectified mid-heaven can be swung backwards and forwards until it connects with one of the planets or some other feature on the chart at the relevant age.

For example, a change in one's direction in life would connect with a progression of the midheaven from one sign to another. An accident might be set off by a midheaven square to Mars or Uranus. Good exam results might be midheaven conjunct, sextile or trine the Sun or Mercury, while a move of house would connect with the Moon, or with a square or opposition if the subject felt it to be an unhappy event, or with a trine or sextile if it was a happy one. A conjunction could go either way. Obviously, this takes a good deal of astrological knowledge, but there are plenty of books on the market which show the effect of planets natally, by progression or when transiting.

Pre-Natal Epoch Birthcharts
A normal pregnancy takes 280 days or 40 weeks, so counting back from the date of birth will take you back to the date of conception. Look at the position of the Moon on the conception date because the theory is that this will be near an angle. I've tried this several times

and it does seem to work. Incidentally, if you have decent software, it will do this for you if you select it.

Simply using this book will help you to get close to the right time of birth, as the person will recognise which Asc, MC, Dsc and IC are theirs. Then, it's only a case of fine tuning the chart by linking events to the movement of the MC or to particular transits on the chart.

25

I 'ave No Ascendant!

Just to show you how weird things can get in astrology, here is the strange tale of Olga, the Russian artist, who Jan and I met several years ago at a gathering of astrologers and psychics in London.

> 'I 'ave no ascendant' breathed the charmingly accented foreign voice in my ear.
> 'What?' I replied in surprise. 'What do you mean, you have no *ascendant*?'
> 'I am Russian and my name is Olga' said the attractive young lady, 'I was born way up in the north of Russia during polar night, and though I 'ave been to many Russian astrologers and even one or two 'ere, nobody has been able to find my ascendant.'

This was certainly an unusual situation and it looked as though Olga might be right. In the popular astrological systems, such as Placidus and Equal House, dropping a line down from sunrise at the birth latitude to the ecliptic forms the ascendant. So, in theory, if there is no sunrise, there can be no ascendant! I said, 'you'd better come and see me and I'll think of something.'

NB: Olga was born on the 21st of January 1963 at 11:10 am local time in Norilsk, Northern Russia.

Olga came for her consultation a couple of weeks later, and as luck would have it, my friend Sean Lovatt happened to phone me while she was there. I told Sean about Olga and he stayed on the line as he entered her details into his computer, while I put her details into mine. Sean and I experimented with various different house systems. Sean tried Campanus and commented that it showed an ascendant of 27 degrees of Virgo. He also muttered darkly that in theory, Olga's ascendant was also her descendant. Sean cut the connection and went off to play with Olga's chart by himself.

The phone rang again and this time my friend Jonathan Dee came on the line. Jon is another very experienced astrologer, and he immediately threw Olga's data into his machine and said that he would ring back if he came up with any bright ideas. Before he rang off, Jon said that he would give Porphyry a try. Meanwhile I got on with trying anything that I could think of.

I discovered that Porphyry only showed four astrological houses, these being the first, sixth, seventh and twelfth. Campanus was better, as it showed a few more shrivelled houses gathered at the MC and the IC. Calls came in from Jonathan and Sean, both saying that they had also discovered that Campanus gave the best results. It was interesting that Sean, Jon and I were all using different software. While none of the programs could cope with this chart, at least they all made exactly the *same* mess of it!

Olga understood the system, but she commented that a Virgo ascendant simply didn't fit any aspect of her life or her personality. I was just coming to the crazy conclusion that Olga's chart was *upside down* when Jon phoned me back to tell me that he had also come to that conclusion! Then Sean phoned to tell me that the chart was not only upside down but also back to front! A Virgo rising chart showed the sun and its close neighbours, Mercury and Venus, in the *lower* hemisphere, but Olga was born at 11.10 am. Even allowing for Polar night, a morning birth couldn't possibly put the sun in the lower hemisphere, i.e. *below* the equator!

For people like us who live in the northern hemisphere, the only way to make sense of an astrology chart is to stand facing the south. Then the midheaven points towards the sun, the ascendant is to the east and the descendant to the west. If I did this with Olga's chart, it showed that the sun was shining on the other side of the earth. Clearly, at that time of the year, it *was* - but this made no astrological sense.

In addition to what was clearly a wrong ascendant, Olga's computer-generated chart showed aspects that weren't actually possible. The nodes of the Moon can only be in opposition to each other, but Olga's were *trine!* The chart bore some resemblance to older types of European charts in which the houses stayed equal and the signs stretched to fit them, but everything on them was all so much out of alignment that it was hard to see what the aspects between the planets really were.

I gave up on the astronomical impossibilities and followed a hunch that Pisces was the probable ascendant - in other words, that the apparent Dsc was actually the Asc. I gave Olga information about the personality and the early life experiences of someone with Pisces rising, and she agreed that this described her childhood and personality. In addition, Olga is a professional artist, which fits a Pisces ascendant. I then rectified the chart to give an ascendant of 27° degrees of Pisces and used the Equal House system. This gave me a workable chart, and it was no hardship to write in the correct position for the moon on both the natal and progressed charts by hand. I then interpreted the chart for Olga in the normal way, taking my time about it and looking at every point in detail. An ecstatic Olga went away with her newly minted ascendant!

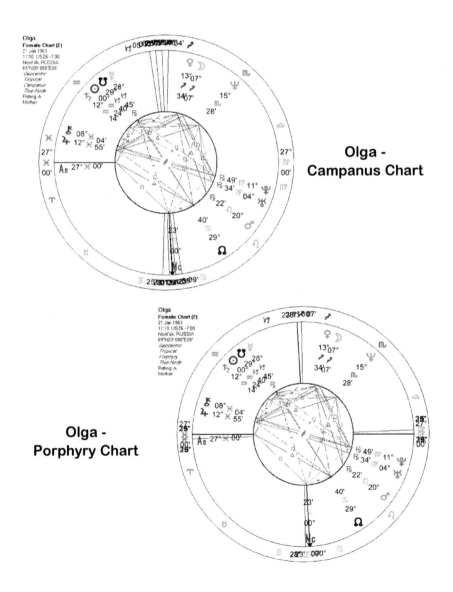

Olga - Campanus Chart

Olga - Porphyry Chart

Additional Data

The equal house chart worked as well as anything could, but see where the MC is - it's at the bottom of the chart! Also, the Vertex is near the Asc, rather than being where it should be, which is in the fifth, sixth, seventh or eight house.

The text in the charts is rather small, so here are the birth details:

Olga was born at 11:10 on the 21st January 1963 in Norilsk, Russia (69 deg. 20 min. North, 88 deg. 06 min. East).

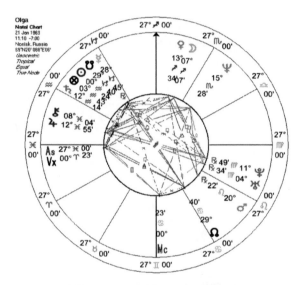

Olga - equal house Chart

26

Some Celebrities in More Detail

Boris Johnson

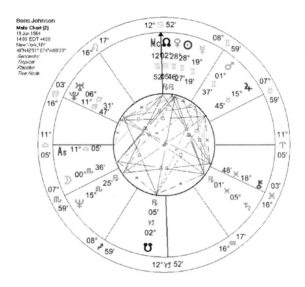

Why do we all love Boris Johnson so much? Did we vote him in as Mayor of London because he is so appealing? Probably.

Boris has Libra rising, and this is the most outwardly charming and loveable rising sign of all, so whatever Boris may be underneath, his Asc alone allows him to make the most of himself, outwardly at least. In his case, he comes across as a cuddlesome, living, breathing, oversized teddy bear. There is a touch of sexiness about our Boris too, because Libra is a sexy Asc. So is his Scorpio Moon, and he has masculine Mars and lucky Jupiter in the sexy eighth house. In theory, this set-up would signify a dark and dangerous looking suave and sexy film star, but mop-haired Boris shambles along and looks a mess. However, women want to tuck his shirt in, brush his hair and mother him. Boris has the Sun, Mercury and Venus in Gemini in the ninth house, so he has a quick and clever brain. This makes him even more interesting to some of us, as we quite like our political leaders to have a bit of brain as well as personality.

Boris was born in New York, of an international background, and he is a member of the British and German Royal Families, albeit on the wrong side of someone's sheets! He says he is the original melting pot, being Turkish, European, and with Jewish, Christian and Muslim antecedents. His international background and appeal is shown by the stellium of planets in his ninth house. Wherever he happened to be born, he takes his responsibility to London and Britain very seriously, and with the Moon as rising planet, along with his Cancerian MC, he is patriotic and protective towards the UK.

He is more sensitive than he looks on the outside, and also more ambitious than he looks. He may act the bumpkin at times and he does make gaffes, but he is quick, clever and well educated. As one would expect with so much Cancer on his chart, he is a knowledgeable historian.

Barack Obama

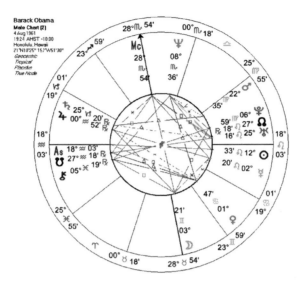

Barack Obama has an international background. He was born in the exotic city of Honolulu in the Hawaiian Islands, which were once British. His father was Kenyan and his mother mid-Western American, but her antecedents were English, Scottish, Irish and Italian. He has a sister living in Germany and other siblings in Africa and elsewhere. He has lived in Indonesia and, somehow, he has an old-world dignity about him that suggests more than a whiff of the now-vanished British Empire.

Barack Obama has Aquarius rising, which makes him a force for change, a revolutionary and a man who can bring about breakthroughs where others face brick walls. The Sun in Leo and his Aquarius Asc make him a determined and stubborn (albeit charming) personality who won't let much get in his way. I am slightly worried about the Scorpio MC, as he would have more luck on his side if it was Sagittarius - but, if that were so, then perhaps he would have settled for Secretary of State for Foreign Affairs rather than go all out for President.

His Sun in the sixth house makes him a hard worker who can cope with details, while the Gemini Moon makes him intelligent and quick-minded, although apt to argue when it isn't always necessary. The friendly Aquarian Asc, Leo Sun and seventh house stellium make him a people person, while the Scorpio MC gives him a touch of much needed gravity.

Michelle Obama

We know that a Capricorn Sun leads to ambition and a tendency to count the pennies, but Michelle's Cancer Asc makes her appear to be the perfect mother. She should have - and indeed does have - a good relationship with her own mother, and she is very close to her children. She could become a kind of 'mother to the nation' in a similar way to Princess Diana and the Queen Mother in the UK. Her MC, Venus, Chiron and Moon in Pisces make her extremely sensitive, romantic and vulnerable, and this adds to her 'Princess Diana' image, but it also makes her somewhat unpredictable.

My guess is that she is tough and capable on the outside, due to her cardinal sign Sun and Asc, but she is gentle, sensitive and easily hurt on the inside. Some may pip her as a future President, but I suspect there isn't enough deep-down hardness in her makeup, and she may also fantasise a little too much, so that, if pushed, she could be caught out in thoughtless exaggerations or silly remarks. She would be a wonderful storyteller or writer of children's books.

Harrison Ford

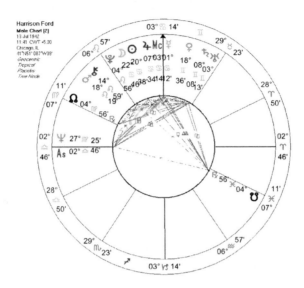

With Libra on the Asc, Harrison's charm and popularity is assured, but he is not as soft as he looks. Libra is a cardinal sign, and his Sun, Moon and MC are all in Cancer, which is also a cardinal sign, so there is no arguing with this man. We know that Harrison was a carpenter before his acting career took off, and that he still relaxes by making furniture; the Cancer stellium would fit with that scenario, as Cancer likes to make things that help to create comfy homes for people.

Cancer is a sign that can create a fantasy in its own mind and then bring it into being. Cancerians really can make the impossible happen, so they are wizard at throwing out an image that may be very different from their real natures. Neptune is close to Harrison's Asc, giving him a rich fantasy life and endowing him with acting ability. This rising planet adds to his attractiveness.

He uses his homely Cancerian image to present himself on-screen as an ordinary man who has become caught up in extra-ordinary situations. The fact that there are no planets below the horizon means that his image and public life are vital to him, but the emphasis on the 'home and family' signs of Gemini, Cancer and Leo make his private life equally important to him.

Angelina Jolie

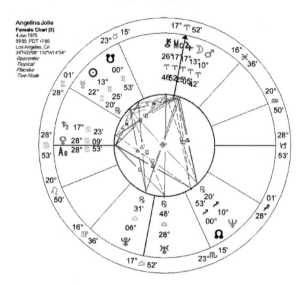

Angelina Jolie's ascendant is almost at the end of Cancer, so the need for home and family life is powerful, but so is the need for recognition. She comes from an acting family, so she has grown up knowing what fame can bring, and this is reflected in the Leo first house. She has to live life to her own drumbeat, though: the cardinal and very self-determined sign of Aries is on her MC, with Jupiter, the Moon and Mars (the ruler of Aries) nearby. Her eleventh house Sun in Gemini makes her quick, clever and rather unusual, and my guess is that she reads a great deal and that she has a mind full of interesting facts and snippets of information. Although Angelina's Cancer ascendant and Venus in Cancer, conjunct the Asc, make her the most feminine of women, she has a muscular intellect. Her Sun in Gemini and Moon, Mars, Jupiter, Chiron and MC in Aries, make her an interesting combination and a complex personality.

Angelina's Moon and stellium in the ninth house make her appeal to all kinds of people, all over the world. Her fabulously aspected Neptune in the fifth house makes her creative and attractive, and being in Sagittarius, it helps her to be agile, strong and sporty.

Some sadness lingers in her twelfth house Saturn, possibly due to a lack of any real education. She may have felt pressure during childhood due to parents who didn't really get on with each other, as shown by her Saturn being square to her Moon, which is a classic case of growing up with parents who were at odds with each other.

Susan Boyle

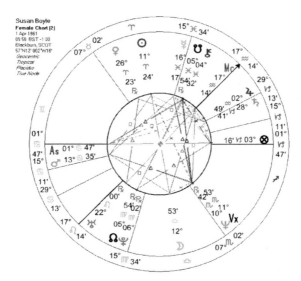

Susan Boyle
Female Chart [2]
1 Apr 1961
09:59 BST -1:00
Blackburn, SCOT
57°N12' 002°W16'
Geocentric
Tropical
Placidus
True Node

On the evening of the 11th of April 2009, in front of millions of people, a phenomenon occurred in the shape of Susan Boyle when she first appeared on the 'Britain's Got Talent' TV programme. So let's start with Susan's natal chart - both for the ascendant's sake as far as this book is concerned, and as a whole, because it's really unusual and fascinating.

Mars rules the brain, and the first house rules the early stages of life, the head, the brain and the body as a whole. In Susan's case, Mars rules her Aries Sun sign. There it sits, in the first house, at the fulcrum of a T-square involving the most personal planets of all - the Sun and the Moon. Mars brought danger to her birth in the shape of oxygen starvation. This affected her brain, making her a slow-learner at school and the victim of bullies. However, this powerful, angular Mars also sits at the leading edge of a grand trine to Mercury and the Neptune/Vertex conjunction, all in sensitive water signs. Susan expresses herself through music, as shown by the link between Mercury (communication) and Neptune (music) for the benefit of others (Vertex). Like a number of Arians and those with Mars rising, she lacks a bit of common sense. She is no beauty, but she has immense beauty in her voice and she was a popular favourite to win the contest. Losing the top spot by a narrow margin was only due to the incredibly strong competition.

Cancer rising suggests a strong bond with the parents, and that is certainly the case for Susan, as she stayed at home and cared for her parents until their death. By her own admission, she is still a virgin who has never been kissed, as shown by the dead weight of Capricorn on the seventh, eighth, and ninth house cusps, and Saturn itself sitting in the eighth house. After her parents died, a lack of opportunities for work and sheer loneliness led her into doing voluntary work for her beloved church. Neptune is well aspected and Jupiter is in her ninth house, both of which indicate benefits from religion. The heavy Saturn and Capricorn situation, especially in the eighth house, shows a huge amount of karma in Susan's life, both in the sense of repaying some massive karmic debt and then gaining massive karmic rewards later in life. For Saturn, life truly does begin at fifty!

So, is there anything in Susan's chart to suggest fame and fortune? Susan's Cancer Asc makes her appear to outsiders as being 'mumsy' rather than looking anything remotely like a modern pop star, but Cancer is a cardinal sign, so it can make things happen when it wants to. Her Aries Sun and Libra Moon are also in cardinal signs, as are her Mars in Cancer (Mars is her Sun's ruler) and the Moon in Libra (the Moon is her chart ruler). This denotes that once she gets herself into gear, very little will stop her. When one of the nodes (preferably the north node) is conjunct Pluto, the person will achieve fame and fortune. In Susan's case, the north node is within a few seconds of an exact conjunction with Pluto.

Progressions

So, what happened on the fateful day? The progressions weren't that amazing, but Susan has been singing for years, so she didn't do anything that she hadn't before, albeit to a larger and more important audience. My guess is that the progressions would have been more interesting when her parents died and when she started her church work, but an Asc progressing into Leo has plenty to say about wanting to be a star.

Progressed Asc into Leo.

Progressed MC trine progressed Asc.

Progressed MC sextile natal Jupiter.

Progressed Dsc conjunct natal Jupiter.

Transits

If some one came to me with a chart that looked like Susan's did at the time of the competition, all I could have said for certain was that the astonishing number of transiting connections showed that something extraordinary was about to occur. When there is this much activity, it is hard to pin it down to any one thing.

Here is a full list of all the aspects involved; it will be most interesting to follow Susan's progress over the next few years, to see just how her life takes shape from now on. It's most unlikely that her past loneliness and lack of opportunities will continue.

Susan Boyle - transit chart aspects on 11th April, 2009

Transiting Sun trine natal Uranus
Transiting Moon trine natal Mercury
Transiting Mercury trine natal Pluto
Transiting Mercury trine natal north node
Transiting Mercury sextile natal south node
Transiting Mercury sextile natal part of fortune
Transiting Mercury square natal Jupiter
Transiting Venus sextile natal Saturn
Transiting Mars inconjunct natal Uranus
Transiting Jupiter opposite natal Uranus
Transiting Saturn opposite natal Mercury
Transiting Saturn sextile natal Mars
Transiting Uranus sextile natal Venus
Transiting Uranus inconjunct natal Uranus
Transiting Neptune opposite natal Uranus
Transiting Neptune semi-sextile natal Saturn
Transiting Chiron semi-sextile natal Saturn
Transiting Chiron opposite natal Uranus
Transiting Pluto conjunct natal part of fortune (exact)
Transiting north node inconjunct natal north node
Transiting south node inconjunct natal south node
Transiting MC opposite natal Saturn
Transiting MC square natal Venus
Transiting IC conjunct natal Saturn
Transiting Asc opposite natal Venus

Phew! What a day for Susan Boyle! Now at last, she can enjoy the progression of her Asc from Cancer to Leo.

27

Conclusion

I wrote the original 'Rising Signs' back in the 1980s, and it was useful for those who were learning about astrology at that time. However, upon looking at it again after a gap of twenty years, it seemed that the original book was somewhat indigestible for a beginner to manage. This time round, I have trimmed the waffle while retaining the essential data for each rising sign. I have added info that I didn't have in those days and this has led to the inclusion of several completely new chapters.

I've included far more about rising sign and midheaven combinations than appeared in the first edition, and I've also dealt more thoroughly with the MC itself, along with the IC and Dsc than I did before, mainly because I've learned more about these things myself in the intervening years. I haven't pulled my punches where certain rising signs or Asc/MC combinations lead to offensive or hurtful behaviour, because I truly believe that people can control this side of themselves if they want to. I believe that they will lead happier lives and have a better karma if they make the effort, and they will certainly make those around them happier.

The rising sign was the first thing that grabbed my attention when I started to learn astrology, and it still fascinates me today. I feel that it's a crying shame that English birth certificates don't include the time of birth in the way that Scottish and American ones do. This leaves so many people floundering around without a proper ascendant until they can discover ways of working out their rising signs by means of rectification, and that is not an easy thing to do.

Whatever your level of interest in astrology, I wish you the very best of pleasure, leisure and luck with your studies.

Index

D

E

F

Zambezi Publishing Ltd

We hope you have enjoyed reading this book. The Zambezi range of books includes titles by top level, internationally acknowledged authors on fresh, thought-provoking viewpoints in your favourite subjects. A common thread with all our books is the easy accessibility of content; we have no sleep-inducing tomes, just down-to-earth, easily digestible, credible books.

~~~~~

Please visit our website (www.zampub.com) to browse our full range of Lifestyle and Mind, Body & Spirit titles, and to discover what might spark your interest next...

~~~~~

Please note:-

Our books are available from good bookshops throughout the UK, but nowadays, no bookshop can hope to carry in stock more than a fraction of the books published each year (over 200,000 new titles were published in the UK last year!). However, most UK bookshops can order and supply our titles swiftly, in no more than a few days (within the UK).

You can also find all our books on amazon.co.uk, other UK internet bookshops, and many are also on amazon.com; sometimes under different titles and ISBNs. Look for the author's name.

Our website (www.zampub.com) also carries and sells our whole range, direct to you. If you prefer not to use the Internet for book purchases, you are welcome to contact us direct (our address is at the front of this book, and on our website) for pricing and payment methods.

Lightning Source UK Ltd.
Milton Keynes UK
21 February 2011

167945UK00001B/165/P